How to Build Self-Esteem and Be Confident

OVERCOME FEARS, BREAK HABITS, BE SUCCESSFUL AND HAPPY

Maddy Malhotra

For Betterment Publications
INCREASING SUCCESS AND HAPPINESS
United States • United Kingdom
Canada • Europe • India

I wasn't born lucky! How to Build Self-Esteem and Be Confident Overcome fears, break habits, be successful and happy

Disclaimer

Every effort has been made to make this book as accurate as possible. However, the text should be used only as a general guide and not as the ultimate source of the subject matter covered. The author shall have neither liability nor responsibility to any person or entity with respect to any loss or damage caused or alleged to be caused directly or indirectly by the information covered in this book.

My Gratitude

To my mentors and coaches.

To my dear friends and family members who believe in me, genuinely care and motivate me.

To my inner-self and my body which has guided me and has been with me every minute of learning, adversity, growing and creating this book.

To the Universe for connecting me with great people and opportunities.

To all the authors, speakers and organizers of all the personal development books, seminars, workshops and courses I have read and attended.

To all my clients who gave me the opportunity to make a difference and to learn and grow.

To all those who, I thought, gave me pain, pushed me down or abused me. They made me stronger and wiser.

And to everyone who has been part of my journey so far...

A Note for You

Thank you for your commitment and investment in personal development. I am going to share some basics of life which I have learned and implemented very successfully in my own life. These philosophies have been followed by every successful person and their roots can also be found in ancient wisdom.

I have attended many life-success and personal development seminars from the best in the world, read more than 100 self-help books and biographies of many successful people. I have interviewed multi-millionaires, performance coaches of top athletes and actors, executives of multi-nationals and even a billionaire. I attended courses for 7 different types of therapies and studied traditional psychology as well. I have gone through hundreds of self-growth articles and ideas of great philosophers and leaders. I was determined to know 'Why we do what we do'. Why only 10% (or less) of us are very successful and/or happy and the majority of the population is struggling for - money, inner-peace, love and joy.

I am going to share the summary of my learning. I have experimented, applied and lived these myself and my clients have benefited from it. I don't want anyone to feel unworthy, unlovable, or incapable so I have revealed some very important facts which can help you live a happier and fulfilled life. These secrets affect every area of our lives every single day but are <u>not</u> taught at school and are rarely a part of parenting! This became the biggest reason for me to write this book and create seminars and home study course.

Along my journey I came across the story of the two wolves (which I'll share with you in chapter 1). For me this simple story sums up our internal battle – the battle between our resourceful beliefs and our limiting beliefs. It summed up the battle that raged within me and around me between the positive and negative beliefs I held about myself and the beliefs that others (parents, family, teachers) held about me. For too long the 'evil' wolf was feasting and the 'good' wolf went hungry!

However, I learned that there are ways of feeding the 'good' wolf and when I started to do that great things started to happen in my life:

The 'mess' started to untangle. It felt like I received answers to the 'puzzle' called life. My quest and hunger to know more of 'how life works', and how to live a life with more happiness, more peace, more satisfaction, began to be fulfilled.

I connected to my inner-self (which is also called the process of 'self-realisation').

I became curious like a child and started exploring all the resources I could to gain more knowledge – inspirational & spiritual seminars, books, videos, articles, audios, movies, forums & communities on the internet, courses etc.

I became more health conscious because I started looking at my body parts as precious and felt gifted. I started enjoying music, dancing on my own and singing out loud!

I started becoming more relaxed and alive with a sense of well being through my whole body. And I started to sleep better (very important!).

Yes, it is possible for you to design and live the life of your dreams and my aim for this book is to make you aware of the elements required for a successful and fulfilled life. The most important of which is a bullet-proof self belief, because that underpins *everything*. You need to believe totally in yourself and your abilities if you are going to achieve anything. Success in any area of life begins in your mind. It's the 'inner' work you need to do first. A hidden lack of self belief is usually what sabotages our efforts.

"Far better is it to dare mighty things, to win glorious triumphs, even though checked by failure... than to rank with those poor spirits who neither enjoy much nor suffer much, because they live in a gray twilight that knows not victory nor defeat." ~Theodore Roosevelt

You don't know what you don't know. While reading this book some of you may think 'what is this guy talking about' and that's understandable because most of us are unaware of these realities about life. Our minds have been programmed otherwise. I can assure you this works. It will be worth the investment. I've been using these techniques for years to re-engineer many aspects of my life.

I would like to thank you for sparing time and congratulate you for taking action, by reading this book. I would love to receive your comments and suggestions.

Maddy

Maddy Malhotra
Success and Happiness Coach,
International Inspirational Speaker

www.CoachMaddy.com

Table of Contents

Let's Go Deep Within

Bonus chapters

Maddy the Hungry Wolf

First, the story:

One evening an old Cherokee told his grandson about a battle that goes on inside people.

He said, 'My son, the battle is between two 'wolves' inside us all. One is *Evil*. It is anger, envy, jealousy, sorrow, regret, greed, arrogance, self-pity, guilt, resentment, inferiority, lies, false pride, superiority, and ego.

The other is *Good*. It is joy, peace, love, hope, serenity, humility, kindness, benevolence, empathy, generosity, truth, compassion and faith.'

The grandson thought about it for a minute and then asked his grandfather: 'Which wolf wins?'

The old Cherokee simply replied, *'The one you feed.'*

My Name is 'Madhur' but people call me 'Maddy'. I grew up in a semi-developed town in the outskirts of Delhi. This town was one of the top three crime areas in India. In my illustrious neighbourhood there was no electricity for up to 12 hours every day. The drinking water was deemed undrinkable by the World Health Organization; there were no water filters and the water was supplied for just an hour a day - if there was an electric supply. There was no air-conditioning when it was 45 degrees and no room or water heaters when it was 5 degrees.

In my town there were no health and safety laws. In our house, the food was cooked in a clay oven or on a kerosene stove throughout my childhood. We did not have the privilege of having access to a telephone, a washing machine or other modern household appliances.

I had no soft toys or electronic gadgets and I was not given any pocket money so I had to fish marbles out of the drain in order to play with other children.

My family was very religious. There was an hour's prayer in the morning and another hour in the evening with visits to the temple as well. We lived in a six bedroom house but there were three families and three couples living in that six bedroom house; all of them were my extended family.

I was never hugged, kissed or praised by my parents because they believed that beating your child was the road to your child's success. The mindset of my family was a mixture of miserliness along with working class and some middle class beliefs. On top of all this my family discriminated against the poor and darker skinned people and that influenced my relations with others then and later in life. Abuse (physical, sexual, mental) was rife in the community I lived in and the close proximity of humans living so tightly together. I have been a victim of communal riots a few times... as a child I remember the sound of bullets and cries of people on our street... we had to climb to the terrace and hide for hours to save our lives..!

I tell you this not for sympathy, but because when you understand my background you can also understand why the 'good' wolf went very hungry for many years. Poverty and deprivation is not just about poor living standards, many suffer from emotional deprivation just because they grew up in a time or place where feeding the 'good' wolf was considered soft or weak, and the way to motivate your child was the stick not the carrot.

My story is not unique in the world, but I found a way to change the probable ending and to rewrite my predicted future, and that is what I want to help you to do too.

Not surprisingly I was a below average student. I was not interested in what they had to teach me. Inevitably I was bullied. I failed in A levels (Grade 11/12) and scored poor grades at the end which, in India, meant I was good for nothing. I will never be successful or happy. I was depressed and suicidal! So... what were my prospects? What could a boy from such an environment expect, or indeed hope for?

Hope is our birthright; and hope, fortunately, springs eternal in the human breast.

English is my third language. I did not speak the Indian version of proper English until I was 22 years old. My relatives who lived in the city referred to me as a 'villager'. This was not a compliment! (Incidentally when I finally reached the UK, I was unable to understand or communicate properly for almost 2 years!) My self-image suffered and the feeling of unworthiness increased each time I spoke incorrectly.

Despite my academic inadequacies, my parents had ambitions for me. Their chief, rather unrealistic, hope was that I would be a doctor of medicine! Or a telecoms engineer.

But I could not, for love nor money, get a place at any university in or around Delhi. I was told this gave a bad name to the family. My poor achievements meant that everyone lost hope in me and I was told that my fate was, horror of horrors, to live a working class life. But I am a fighter and against the odds, I confounded them by enrolling for a degree at the Open University…

Despite working hard at my course, I failed 3 semesters and the pressure from my parents continued. The mind games they played reinforced in them (and often in me) their notions that I was a failure and would never be able to lead a contented and abundant life. My already low self-esteem plummeted.

An additional pressure was that the extended family in India thinks it is their right to chip in with their negative forecasts and expectations. I was forced to be more religious than I wished and to do what astrologers and priests told me. I became bowed down by the limiting, negative beliefs of the very society in which I lived.

Boy, was that 'evil' wolf having a feast! But still there remained a driving force within me to prove my worth and to prove them wrong! The 'good' wolf was starving but he was determined to survive!

3

So I did something that surprised them all. Talk about burning your bridges! At the age of 23 with my frustration steadily increasing, I decided to leave my country for good. I took out a loan of, what was for me, the enormous sum of $8,000! This was for a diploma in customer service management in a place called Nottingham. 'Where is Nottingham?' I thought. I had also managed to save, by leading a non-existent social life for eight years, the princely sum of $380 for living expenses.

Now, I did not really know what the UK was. I knew the names London, Britain and England and now I knew of Nottingham. All I really knew was that I desperately wanted to leave India and migrate to a developed country. I was flying to London - I was going to England!!

This was a period of many 'firsts' for me - first time away from home, first visa, first time at an airport and on an airplane. A lot for our village boy to deal with!

My arrival in the UK was a huge cultural and technological shock. I did not know anyone in the UK. My $380 saved over eight years lasted me for less than eight days - quite an achievement!

Throughout my diploma course I was forced to work part time to survive. For the first three months I worked as a dishwasher at a restaurant. That was a big dent in my self-esteem.

For the first 11 months in the UK I could afford only two meals a day. At one time I was doing two part-time jobs a day. Then I landed a job in a call centre and this sustained me until the course finished.

The added pressure and challenge was the knowledge that no one in India supported me, or believed in me. My parents predicted that I would return a failure, my tail between my legs, having wasted the money I had borrowed. I should point out that the loan of $8,000 in India represented two years salary for an accountant or doctor at that time. But...I managed to pay off that loan after only 2 years in England! And then left my job in the call centre and burnt my bridges again!!

I borrowed a further $9,000 to pursue a specialist course in Computer Networking in London. Whilst studying for this course I continued to live on the fringes of society, constantly borrowing from very good friends just to get by. There were drugs, alcohol, gambling and prostitution present in the house I lived in, a constant and depressing backdrop to this period.

I was fortunate or unfortunate enough, on the 7th July 2005, to be on one of the tube trains which was found to have a bomb, (unexploded)!! Was luck on my side or just teasing me?

And each year the application for the Visa extension was ever more stressful! It seemed so hard to swim against the current towards the open sea. I sometimes felt I was merely treading water.

I asked myself : had that 'village' boy, back in India, been foolish to have his dreams and hopes? Was he heading out of the frying pan and into the fire?

Then, after all that studying, debt and hardship, in August 2005 I got a good Job with British Telecom in Sheffield. I once again applied for my visa and received one of the 'Highly Skilled' variety!

YES! Life was getting better now that I had a full time job. My confidence and self esteem grew and flourished. The news came from India that the parents and the extended family were pleased; they were prepared to rejoice with me in my achievements and good fortune. I paid off all my loans, opened a savings account, and could afford better food, luxuries and clothes. A lesson had been well learned about life's possibilities! My 'good' wolf was getting a few morsels at last.

But as time passed, nagging doubts grew. There had to be more to life than financial security and physical well being. I had anticipated that attaining worldly success would bring me the happiness I longed for. When achieving this success failed to deliver happiness, I sought it elsewhere.

In 2007 I attended my first motivational seminar and read my first self-help book and then attended and read many more led and written by the best in the world.

My previously religious mindset changed to a more spiritual one. A transformation gradually occurred and my beliefs began to change. Life was full of possibilities! I could plan my own destiny and get rid of limiting beliefs... I felt I was exploring and becoming connected to myself. At last my mind was clear and positive.

Alongside my full time job I completed courses in life coaching, NLP (Neuro-Linguistic Programming), hypnotherapy and psychology. And I have attempted to implement the knowledge in myself... I have made an effort to

- ✓ **change my limiting beliefs**
- ✓ become aware and take control of my **thoughts and emotions**
- ✓ forgive myself and others,
- ✓ start loving myself,
- ✓ be thankful for all that I have - even for the pain I had, in the past
- ✓ and smile more often

I have studied successful leaders and have noted their strengths and techniques and attempted to model them.

With all this new study, I began to write like crazy. I used to wake up in the middle of the night and start writing. There was a flow of inspiration and power from within me. And I started writing about attaining Happiness and Peace in the 21st century.

So, professionally, I had achieved a level of success every Indian parent would like their child to have reached, a level most of the top graduates from India would want to have reached; and I was doing pretty well by British standards too! I worked for a prestigious organisation, earning 100 times more than I used to five years ago!

Do you sense the familiar aroma of burning bridges? You are right to! I took another big step and quit my day job to fulfil my passion.

In the past many people commented that I was 'too happy and peppy for my own good. That I didn't take my responsibilities seriously enough'. But I always knew my natural joy and energy were, and are, my greatest strengths. I am well placed and on the brink of achieving my dream.

I had an option to buy a house, start a business (franchisee) or even invest in share market but I chose to invest my savings in myself. It was a tough decision, involved many calculations and I had to deal with fear of financial security and fear of failure. Since 2007 I have invested over $40,000 in personal development. My colleagues and friends thought I had lost the plot when I disclosed that. ☺

I decided to learn from the best mentors in the world. My learning continues and I am hungry to know more about life, and understand why we do what we do. I am constantly attempting to get my hands on more tools and techniques through which I can live a better life and share my knowledge with others so that they can too.

I have had one-to-one coaching with the best mental toughness coach in the world and had a personal life coach for a year. I am a certified NLP practitioner, Hypnotherapist, time-change-therapy practitioner and hold a diploma in psychology. I have also taken a course in psychotherapy/TA at the **University of Oxford** and in Cognitive Behavioural Therapy and Rational Emotive Behaviour Therapy. Learning coaching skills, both personal and professional, at the prestigious **University of Cambridge** was insightful. I also support university students in the UK and South Asia for their thesis/research work related to positive psychology.

I have been a volunteer for various charities and NPOs for the past few years. Whether its polio eradication & AIDS awareness for the UNICEF or teaching life skills (mentioned in this book) to young orphans in India or the projects for the Red Cross, it has always been a nice and fulfilling experience. My motivation increased when I received a certificate of appreciation from the **Queen of England**, an award from the Mayor of Sheffield, from a president of Lion's club and the High Sheriff of South Yorkshire. I was also invited for a lunch with the Queen's youngest son **Prince Edward** and his wife Sophia.

I have been a regular guest on radio and have been interviewed by stations worldwide including, multiple times on, the **BBC**. I've done motivational shows for well-being TV channels and have been featured in several national newspapers, health magazines and high ranking websites/blogs. I feel so happy when I see my motivational quotes regularly shared on the social media, authors use them in their books and are impacting the corporate world.

I am thankful for all that I have. Happiness, contentment, bliss, peace and gratitude are part of my daily life now. My good wolf is fed and flourishing. The 'evil' wolf is now the one who is hungry.

And so I would like to share with you some of the amazing things I have learnt on this journey. Some things you might be familiar with and some things may be as much a surprise to you as they were to me. Either way, your 'good' wolf will be grateful for the nourishment, and ultimately so will you.

"I am not a teacher, only a fellow traveller of whom you asked the way. I pointed ahead – ahead of myself as well as you."
~George Bernard Shaw

"Winners never quit and quitters never win." ~Vince Lombardi

Work harder on yourself than you do your job. For things to change you've got to change. For things to get better you've got to get better. Don't wish it was easier, wish you were better. ~Jim Rohn

Life in the 21ˢᵗ Century

Are you living or surviving or fighting or coping?

With advanced technology this is the most comfortable and easy life humans have lived in the past few centuries but mentally the 21st century seems to be the worst time to live. We are more stressed mentally than we have ever been. Why?

We are facing a mental health pandemic – all of us suffering from poor mental health at some point in our lives. We think of mental health being something that affects other people. But actually it affects everyone. The World Health Organisation defines mental health as 'a state of well-being in which every individual realizes his or her own potential, can cope with the normal stresses of life, can work productively and fruitfully, and is able to make a contribution to her or his community. It's a state of complete physical, mental and social well-being and not merely the absence of disease or infirmity.'

How many of us would say that we feel constantly in a 'state of complete physical, mental and social well-being'? Or that we even achieve it some of the time?

Depression is increasingly common – and can strike anyone at anytime. By the year 2020, depression will be the second most common health problem in the world. And that's just one type of mental health issue.

> *"Mental health problems do not affect three of four out of every five persons, but one out of one." ~Dr. William Menninger*

Stress is the most common issue and is ignored by many of us. Research has proven that negative emotions associated with stress such as anxiety, fear, lack of forgiveness, anger, envy etc (all those 'evil wolf' traits!) can cause the release of chemicals (neuropeptides released by the brain) that could lead to poor digestion, irregular heartbeat, high blood pressure and inflammation of the body parts, ulcer, pains, skin diseases, IBS, panic attacks. And this can lead to major illnesses like

11

cancer, depression, diabetes, heart disease. Knowing that why would you want to allow stress to take over?

PsychoNeuroImmunology suggests that hormones such as adrenaline and cortisol (helpful when required) are released in unexpected amounts when a person experiences negative emotions. Such chemicals weaken the immune system. They become toxic for our body and can cause our bodies to create toxic cells which cause dis-ease.

Can you imagine all the diseases or illnesses you are prone to if your immune system is weak or disabled?

On the contrary, positive emotions such as laughter, fulfilment, contentment etc. can make the brain release chemicals which can strengthen the immune system and help an individual to prevent and/or heal cancer and other illnesses. What a relief!

"People are about as happy as they make up their minds to be."
~Abraham Lincoln

People these days are so busy in the rat race of professional growth and earning money that they forget to allocate time and energy for experiencing these positive emotions; finding time and energy for their loved ones, for their peace of mind, for relaxation, for hobbies, for travelling, for fitness, to connect with themselves, to be thankful for what they have, to even celebrate their achievements!

A birthday in the family, anniversaries, public holidays and in some cases vacations - are these the only days when we must feel happy?

Facebook now has more than 1,000,000,000 users and has been measuring how happy or satisfied with life the citizens of a nation are as part of the Gross National Happiness Movement (2013). You can see the graph for your country.

Their data is drawn from the use of what they term positive and negative words posted on Facebook updates. The graphs show a sad picture. Either happiness has become an occasional thing for most of people (users are mostly happy only around public holidays) or we use Facebook for complaining more than we do for spreading our happiness among our friends. Have we lost the happiness habit?

Sure we all have problems, such as:

1) Finances – in debt, just getting by, no savings..

2) Physical Health – overweight, pains..

3) Relationships – living like housemates, occasional love making, lack

of time/commitment..

4) Mental Health –

a) Self – low self-esteem, negative self-image, lack of confidence..

b) Emotions – stress, anxiety, fears, frustration, guilt, worry, anger,

depression, envy, jealousy..

And we deal with these problems in a variety of ways (some more crippling than others):

Smoking, alcohol, emotional eating, drugs, self-harm, pain killers, emotional spending abusing others, getting a pet, producing a baby, becoming a perfectionist to prove our worth, becoming a victim/passive… and a lot of people fool themselves by distracting themselves, ignoring their problems and by suppressing their emotions!

And what are the consequences of using such coping mechanisms? *More problems!!*

Unfortunately most of the treatments or solutions available to us deal with the effects of the problem not the cause. Despite billions of dollars (or £pounds) being poured into the health sector, much of it is directed at treating symptoms not at finding the root cause of the problem. But we don't have to wait for governments to change their focus. **We can start to change it for ourselves and within ourselves.**

We can't solve the problem by focusing on and worrying about the problem itself (feeding the 'evil' wolf!). We need to focus on what is positive in our lives and find the solutions from there.

The following chapters will help you do just that: understand your thinking that is creating problems in your life and changing your thinking to create solutions and find a better life. There are questions at the end of each chapter which will help you explore yourself and your thoughts.

"No problem can be solved from the same level of consciousness that created it." ~Albert Einstein

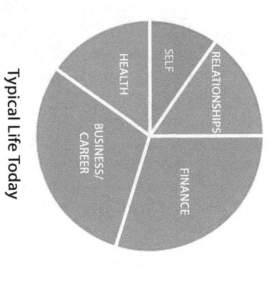

Typical Life Today

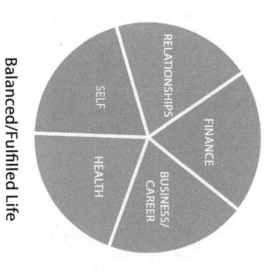

Balanced/Fulfilled Life

15

Explore Yourself

How many times a day do you use these words or feel happy, I can, joyful, possible, thankful, confident, peaceful, delighted, excellent, cheerful, fantastic, proud, love, great, celebrate and enjoyed/enjoying?

Versus

How many times a day do you use these words or feel stressed, anxious, frustrated, need a break, f**king hell, angry, blaming yourself/life/others, depressed, worried, unlucky, sad, fear/fearful, not good enough, rubbish, sh*t, thoughts of lack or scarcity, negative assumptions or doubts?

What does this tell you about the quality of life you are living right now?

What's the logic in having a prestigious job or an established business but lack of emotional fulfilment, physical health issues and/or relationship problems? Is your life balanced?

Why can't we be as happy and lively every evening as we are on a Friday?

Do we need a tag/label for a day of the year to celebrate it? Why do we celebrate our birth only once a year?

YOUR NOTES

It is remarkable how much mediocrity we live with, surrounding ourselves with daily reminders that the average is acceptable. Our world suffers from terminal normality. Take a moment to assess all of the things around you that promote your being 'average'. These are the things that keep you powerless to go beyond a 'limit' you arbitrarily set for yourself. ~Stewart Emery

What They Didn't Teach You about Success and Happiness

Most of us are NOT aware of the facts of life which affect us every single minute!

Have you ever wondered why things don't happen the way they should? Why is it so difficult to live a life of our dreams? Why so some people seem to be lucky while most of us live a life of mediocrity? Some people seem to be happy all day long, are wealthy and enjoy their life more than the majority of us. Why?

A sad truth is that most of us don't know what we really believe! We don't know how we operate. We don't know what is holding us back. We don't know why we do what we do. Why do we like some things and dislike others? What makes us decide right and wrong?

To learn how to read and write we go to school, to learn a profession we often go to a college or university, to learn any technical skills we get trained. Why don't we learn about the mental health (our thoughts, emotions and beliefs) which affects every minute of our lives? Why don't we study and set goals for our relationships? Why don't we make an effort to learn about the ways to create a healthy self-esteem? Where is the school for learning positive mental health? (Actually it is right here – read on!)

Parenting, emotional wellness, love making… do we assume we know it all or we let our lives run on autopilot?

> *"You may know how to operate computers. You may know a lot about aliens or robots. You may be a doctor, lawyer, engineer, teacher, specialist… BUT if you don't know how you operate, why your life is the way it is and how to increase fulfillment, love and peace in your life then all the knowledge and degrees aren't much worth having!"*
> *~Maddy Malhotra*

Today, the word 'success' is understood as having lots of money, material things and/or fame but that's success in only one or two areas of life. What about the other areas? What about our health, happiness and relationships?

Remember, you DO need to work on and give your time and energy to your relationships, physical health, personal development, mental health, spirituality and fun and recreation in order to succeed, **or else you will have the money but no love, joy, peace or fulfilment.**

Money is a must. We all need it to survive, BUT it is no substitute for love, joy, peace and fulfilment. We need these to ensure we thrive as well as survive.

We are born with everything we need to be happy often, to be rich, to have a loving soul mate, to have a healthy body, to be confident. But no one taught us how to access these powers and abilities from within us. No one taught us the psychology of success, of happiness, of love. We can learn it though, and it is never too late to do so.

We are all born in a world full of illusion, people sleepwalking. May be that is why ancient wisdom and the spiritual gurus alive ask us to 'awaken'. Self-realisation, self-awakening, self-awareness takes us to the peak of positive emotions and full control on our lives.

"If most of us remain ignorant of ourselves, it is because self-knowledge is painful and we prefer the pleasures of illusion." ~Aldous Huxley

Why you do what you do? (Your decisions, choices, dislike, like, procrastination, right or wrong, things you know are bad or harmful for you but still do them)

Why you are where you are in your life? (Success or failure in each area of life, depressed or happy, fit or overweight, in a loving relationship or not, low self-esteem or high)

What is stopping you from living the life of your dreams? (Things you wish to have/own in every area of your life but you don't have them)

Self-pity in its early stages is as snug as a feather mattress. Only when it hardens does it become uncomfortable. ~Maya Angelou

Your Biggest Barrier to Success and Happiness

Most of us are victims of self-sabotage (unconsciously).

That's right. Most of us are getting in our own way to earning more money, getting fit, feeling happy, loving ourselves and others!!

Our relationship with ourselves is the most important relationship in our lives and if that relationship isn't love-full, joy-full and peace-full - if we aren't our own best friends - then we must not expect to live a success-full and fulfilled life.

Your opinion about yourself (i.e. how capable you are, how much success and happiness you can achieve, what you deserve and your self-worth) affects your relationships, profession, health, performance and your self-esteem.

Most of us don't love ourselves. We keep giving love to others but rarely to ourselves! And that is just keeping your 'good' wolf hungry!

Think of how many times do you say 'I love you' to others? And now count the no. of times you say it to yourself?

Another enemy of ours or I must say the most useless of all human emotions is Self-Pity. It is addictive. It may give us momentary pleasure but it separates us (victim) from reality! I used to waste my time and harm my body (inducing unhealthy emotions) by feeling sorry for myself, but not anymore.

Do you feel sorry for yourself? Misery won't help you make your life better. Successful people have described self-pity as poison for life and a barrier to success.

The questions you ask when you feel hopeless, such as:

Why me? Why my life? Why does this happen to me?

Who answers them? What answer do you get?

You may have had bad experiences during childhood, may be your parents divorced, you were bad at academic subjects, you lived in poverty, you were abused....

So what?

Are there people who had similar problems in their past or even worse problems than yours who are now rich, happy, love-full, confident and thankful?

Yes! There are many examples, including me.

> *"All blame is a waste of time. No matter how much fault you find with another, and regardless of how much you blame him, it will not change you. The only thing blame does is to keep the focus off you when you are looking for external reasons to explain your unhappiness or frustration. You may succeed in making another feel guilty about something by blaming him, but you won't succeed in changing whatever it is about you that is making you unhappy." ~Dr. Wayne Dyer*

Do you tell yourself: I will be happy when I do/achieve X Y Z?

If you think that you will start enjoying life or you will be happy or proud 'when' or 'if only' you have a million dollars in your bank, or once you buy a nice car or the day you move into your dream house or the day you have a degree or the day you have a perfect soul mate or the day you have your own business or a high designation job... then you are missing out. You don't have to wait. **Happiness, peace, love and pride come from within. You have the choice of feeling happy anytime and anywhere you wish.**

> *"If you keep running away from yourself then be warned that love, joy, peace and fulfilment will keep running away from you!" ~Maddy Malhotra*

Most of us learn to evaluate our self-worth by comparing and competing which is why we have a tendency to compare ourselves with

24

our friends, co-workers, family members and so on. Sadly, this is the root cause of much of the emotional pain that we experience.

Because most of us have a low self-belief and self-esteem (includes self image, confidence, love, worth) we are addicted to the approval of others. We have a fear of being judged or rejected. We are, often, worried about what 'they' will think about us. Our happiness and worth is dependent on 'their' approval.

"If you compare yourself to others, you may become vain and bitter; for always there will be greater and lesser persons than yourself."
~Max Ehrmann

A well known speaker started off his seminar by holding up a $100 bill. In the room of 200, he asked, "Who would like this $100 bill?"

Hands started going up.

He said, "I am going to give this $100 to one of you but first, let me do this." He proceeded to crumple the dollar bill up.

He then asked, "Who still wants it?"

Still the hands were up in the air.

"Well," he replied, "What if I do this?" And he dropped it on the ground and started to grind it into the floor with his shoe.

He picked it up, now all crumpled and dirty. "Now who still wants it?" Still the hands went into the air.

My friends, you have all learned a very valuable lesson. No matter what I did to the money, you still wanted it because it did not decrease in value. It was still worth $100.

In our lives, we are dropped, crumpled, and ground into the dirt by the decisions we make and the circumstances that come our way.

We feel as though we are worthless. But no matter what has happened or what will happen, you will never lose your value. You are special - Don't ever forget it!

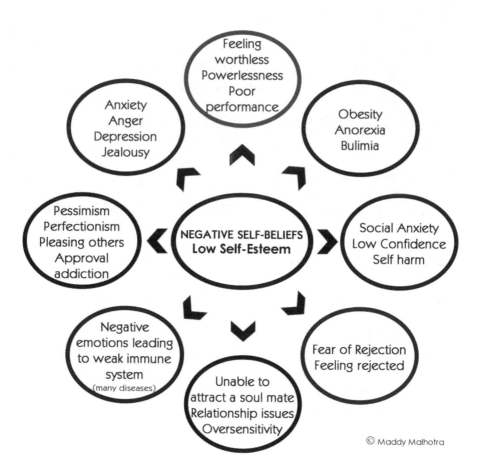

Do you think you are unlucky?

Do you think no one can ever truly love you?

Do you think you don't deserve a happy life?

Do you think you can never be rich?

Do you think your fate is to be abandoned?

Have you accepted unhappiness as your fate?

Do you think life can't always be happy?

How many times a day do you say/think negative things about yourself and/or your life?

Vs

How many times a day do you appreciate yourself and/or recognise your achievements?

How many times a day you blame your fate and/or others for all the problems in your life?

Whom do you hold responsible for your life?

YOUR NOTES

YOUR NOTES

It is that constant daily programming you receive that determines your mindset. And it is your mindset that determines your eventual level of achievement in everything you do. ~Randy Gage

You Were Programmed to Fail

Most of us live by someone else's script; like a pre-programmed robot.

Is it the physical disability which stops people? NO.

There are disabled people who are scientists, motivational speakers, marathon runners, engineers...

Is it lack of education which stops people? NO.

A lot of billionaires and multi-millionaires don't have a degree.

Is it lack of finances which stops people? NO.

Many successful entrepreneurs (including billionaires) weren't born rich or lost all their assets and were in debt at some point.

Most of the people who attend money-making courses don't make much money. Why?

Most of the people who attend motivational seminars slip back to their comfort zone after a week or two. Why?

Goal setting or New Year resolutions don't last for long. Why?

Why is it?

It's because of our BELIEFS.

Your beliefs are the blueprint of your reality. It is referred to as a script or a life plan in Transactional Analysis (an integrative approach to psychology and psychotherapy).

"A belief is assuming something to be true, to be a fact. A belief is not caused, it is created by choice. A belief about a thing's existence is not the same as its existence." ~Bruce Di Marsico

If you don't have the successful career or business that provides the money, fulfilment and freedom, the loving and joyful relationships you desire, the ideal body shape or weight, high self-esteem or self confidence, it's all because of your beliefs!!

Unfortunately most of our intense beliefs are NOT created by us consciously! They are someone else's beliefs which we act upon and defend! **Very few of us examine our beliefs critically. We unconsciously live our lives with beliefs that were, and are, programmed or conditioned into us by others** (parents, teachers, family, bosses, even friends and colleagues).

It's not your fault. And to an extent it isn't theirs either! Most of the people you rely on and learn from including your parents, school/college teachers, community leaders, GPs (medical Doctors), finance consultants, bank managers, don't know about these facts of life either!!

"In medical school, we have a hundred classes that teach us how to fight off death and not one lesson in how to go on living." ~Dr. Meredith Grey

Beliefs start forming the day you were born (some studies reveal they can even be created while you were in the womb). Since then your mind has been recording everything (images, sounds, feelings, tastes and smells) and storing it at a subconscious level.

Various studies show different age groups for this process. In general, the first five to seven years are the most critical for belief formation. The process continues until 15-18. During and after that, usually, we keep repeating what we have been programmed for and form new beliefs with our experiences or verify our old beliefs each time we get a reference to prove them right.

Warning! Our subconscious mind is NOT rational i.e. it can't evaluate whether a belief is good for you or not. It just stores whatever you allow in. Your subconscious will just keep feeding that 'evil' wolf if that is the food you are giving it.

Those beliefs/programs/scripts/blueprints which were created in the first few years of your life (when you didn't even have the ability to question what your mind was recording) are still there and affecting your feelings, attitudes, decisions and actions every day!

Teachers, parents, celebrities and other leaders are, usually, children's role models. If most of these people don't know the power of beliefs, the basic emotional needs and how the life can be made happier, peaceful and love-full, then what are the kids going to learn?

Parents or guardians make us live as per their values, rules and beliefs. Most of them don't know that unconsciously they are conditioning/programming a child's mind. Even when we have grown up and left home, we continue to live 'their' beliefs and perform up to the expectations they had of us during our childhood.

We keep doing what they wanted us to do and keep on believing that all that they told us was right. And we rarely question those beliefs!

This programming is the biggest reason why we have low self-esteem/self-confidence/self-love/self-image; why we can't achieve much and sabotage our success unconsciously; why we don't feel fulfilled; why some of us are passive; why we become perfectionists; why we never experience complete peace of mind; why others are more important than our self, which makes us feel guilty irrationally, which tells us we aren't good enough and the list goes on...

Negative programming of mind, repetition with intense negative emotions or abuse, blame and reminders of the mistakes a child has made, comparison with siblings or their friends, and then labelling or telling the child how stupid, doomed, bad, a failure, a loser, useless, ugly (or any other abusive words) he/she is, makes the child believe it and unconsciously the child keeps believing, living and proving the negative labels, given to her/him, all her/his life.

Most of us were programmed for lack and limitations!

Hopefully this tells you why you are the way you are! The good news is you don't have to continue believing it!

Learned behaviour
Learned behaviour can be defined as the behaviour we learn through our environment.

If the kids see their parents drinking or smoking often then they may create a belief that these stimulants are a part of life and it's ok to consume.

If the kids have heard their parents saying Friday/Saturday night out is fun and the kids see them getting drunk and using positive words for their experience then kids will tend to do the same.

If the kids have seen their parents fighting/arguing/abusing each other, or if one parent is abusing or controlling the other, then what type of beliefs will they create around relationships?

I know many university students who use stimulants for social anxiety or they have a belief to 'enjoy' life as much as they can now. Where do they learn all this?

In Britain, kids are programmed to relate negative emotions and abusive words with rain. Without thinking about it consciously the grown up kids then use the same language and add misery to their lives!

Can you change or control the weather? If not then accept it and reprogram your reaction. Try being grateful for the rain even, some countries need it so badly and don't get any.

Thermostat/Set Point

A lot of overweight people who lose weight gain it back within two years. Why?

Up to 80% of lottery winners loose almost everything they win and slip back to where they were within seven years after winning. Why?

Why do people come close to success or a promotion and then give up or quit or do something weird or decline their performance/progress?

Most of the time, we don't know why we sabotage our success or happiness. We do this unconsciously because of the beliefs we hold for every area of our lives, which make us stay/feel within a certain range.

In his book *Psycho-Cybernetics,* Dr. Maxwell Maltz has compared the human mind to a thermostat. The book talks about the concept of self-image and how it guides everything in our lives.

This thermostat is also called 'set level' or 'set point' by other professionals. If we don't consciously change the set-levels for our income, happiness, self-image, relationships or success in any area of our lives, we keep living in our pre-defined comfort zone. This mechanism is good because it won't let you remain below your set-level unless you choose to, but the bad side is that it will *not* let you rise above your set-level, either!

An example:
Let's say that your ideal weight is 60 kg. So, if you gain weight and weigh 80 kg, you will likely start doing some exercise, go to a gym or on a diet. On the other hand, if you lose some weight and weigh 50 kg, you will likely do things to gain some weight to get back to your set-point. The only way you can change that 60 kg mark is if you accept the new weight and change your self-image (beliefs/rules) to match the new weight/shape.

We do the same for our performance at school, in career/business, and for the levels of our self-esteem and happiness.

That uneasiness we feel when we try to change our habits or try to do something new is our thermostat saying, "You are stepping out of your set-level/comfort zone. Step back to feel secure/better!" A part of our brains is responsible for keeping us safe and secure, but without discomfort and without taking risks, it's highly unlikely that you will create the life of your dreams. Reprogramming/reconditioning of your thermostat is required to progress in life.

What are Doubts? Assumptions? Fears? Worries? Limitations? Excuses?

They are our beliefs and exist only in our mind and they have a negative effect on our feelings, decisions and results in every area of our lives including our physical health!

Are you aware of the term 'placebo'? Patients are given inactive substance like a sugar pill, distilled water or saline solution rather than the real drugs. Patients still improve merely because of their **belief** about the effect of the medicine!

When you say something like 'I have a bad memory', 'I am not/never organised', 'I have a bad habit of ___', 'I have been doing ___ for years', you are reinforcing that habit/behaviour/belief in your mind and so you continue to do/be the same.

Who programmed or continuously programs us?
✓ Parents/Guardian
✓ Extended family/Relatives
✓ Media – TV, Radio, Newspapers, Magazines, Books, Internet (especially news, songs, movies)
✓ Politicians, Religious or Community leaders and other authority figures in life
✓ Teachers, Friends, Classmates, Colleagues and other people whom you spend time with
✓ Advertising banners, posters, t-shirts, stickers, mugs etc
And we do it to ourselves!

Warning! Be aware of whom you spend time with or what do you read, watch or listen.

Have you seen the movie or the read the book called The Secret?

Many personal development speakers, teachers and life-coaches suggest their clients should 'look in the mirror and say good things' about themselves, some suggest affirmations, some prescribe applying the Law of Attraction. These are techniques that work if you **truly believe** those good things or affirmations. But if you say them without believing them, nothing will change. Without dealing with your underlying limiting beliefs, it's impossible to achieve success, happiness and peace of mind.

Did you know that elephants are the strongest land mammals in the world? They are so powerful that a male elephant can lift a 300 kg tree log with his trunk.

A man went to a circus and as he was passing by some elephants, he suddenly stopped, confused by the fact that these big creatures were being held by only a small rope tied to their front leg. It was obvious that the elephants could, at anytime, break away from their bonds but for some reason, they did not.

He approached a trainer and asked why these animals just stood there and made no attempt to break away. The trainer said: when they are very young and small, we use the same size rope to tie them and, at that age, it's enough to hold them. They try to break free but fail. Years later, even though the elephants grow bigger and stronger, they don't even attempt to pull the rope because were conditioned to believe they cannot break away.

The elephants are trapped by their own beliefs!

Do you think elephants have the potential to break a rope? Of course, they have the strength to even pull a tree down!

It may sound strange, the same thing happens to most of us! We have the potential to achieve the success and happiness we want but we go through life holding on to limiting beliefs, for our abilities, simply because we failed in the past. How many of us don't even try something new or challenging?

Failure is a part of learning and growing. Is there anyone who never failed and only succeeded?

Three beliefs that consistently make people less happy and successful -

1. Self worth is based on what others think of me - when we are convinced that others think we aren't good, we lack the confidence and motivation necessary to take consistent action.

2. Past equals future / I am not good enough - many of us assume that our goals are not achievable when we experience setbacks, because of the negative self-beliefs we created after failures in the past. Over time, we become discouraged and avoid situations where failure is a risk.

3. I must do things perfectly - perfection is unattainable hence the ones who seek it simply set themselves up for disappointment. Perfectionists blame others rather than doing what's necessary to accomplish unusual results. Perfectionism, usually, is a result of low self-esteem and is called an illness by many successful people.

Do you have any of these in your mind? Promise yourself to delete these right now!

"To remain fit you must be strong mentally not just physically. That for me is the key." ~Hrithik Roshan
(Celebrated Actor, Sexiest Man in Asia 2015, Inspirational Youth Leader, Philanthropist, Wax figure at Madame Tussauds London)

---

*BBC's website published a research done by some experts from the Cognitive Behaviour department at the University of Oxford. In a nutshell it tells you that the beliefs/perception formed in the early years are responsible for low self-esteem leading to depression, anxiety, fears and other mental health issues.

Explore Yourself

How many beliefs have you got, which work against you?

How many hours of negative/limiting programming do you have each day versus reading self-help books, attending seminars and positive self-talk/affirmations?

Today why would you believe the negative labels you were given at 13? Have you not learnt more, experienced more or done more since then? So if you aren't at the same level as you were at 13 then why would you have the same self-image/worth/confidence?

If I ask you to write 50 achievements of your life, what is the first thought that comes to your mind? Usually people say 'I can't even think of 10' because their head is full of negative beliefs about themselves and they are always blaming themselves for all the mistakes and failures from the past. People usually come up with more than 50 when asked to change their focus and rethink! So go ahead and see how many achievements you can think of.

YOUR NOTES

YOUR NOTES

YOUR NOTES

We are what we think. All that we are arises with our thoughts. With our thoughts, we make our world. ~Buddha

Do You Think Like The Successful Do?

Most of us, everyday, have a lot more negative or disempowering thoughts than positive ones.

Remember the two wolves?

Here's a reminder of the story:

One evening an old Cherokee told his grandson about a battle that goes on inside people. He said, 'My son, the battle is between two 'wolves' inside us all. One is 'Evil'. It is anger, envy, jealousy, sorrow, regret, greed, arrogance, self-pity, guilt, resentment, inferiority, lies, false pride, superiority, and ego.

The other is 'Good'. It is joy, peace, love, hope, serenity, humility, kindness, benevolence, empathy, generosity, truth, compassion and faith.'

The grandson thought about it for a minute and then asked his grandfather: 'Which wolf wins?'

The old Cherokee simply replied, 'The one you feed.'

Have you ever considered exploring what you focus on during your day? What type of thoughts cross your mind? Which of those thoughts are repetitive? Are they negative or positive? Which wolf are you feeding?

What do you think about yourself, others, your ability, about life in general, about what is possible in future and about the world as a whole?

If the answers to the questions above are more negative than positive, like most of us, then you may never be able to live the life of your dreams. WHY?

It's because of this powerful fact which may surprise you or make you think… **Our thoughts become our physical reality!!**

We live in the world, of our thoughts, all day long. The amount of happiness, success, love, peace and fulfilment you experience and achieve depends on the nature and quality of your thoughts.

Either you must control your thoughts or the outside forces will control them and be warned that the outside forces are usually negative (limiting, fearful, worry, doubts, disempowering...)

Control your thoughts, focus on what's important and you may get better results.

"A man's mind may be likened to a garden, which may be intelligently cultivated or allowed to run wild; but whether cultivated or neglected, it must, and will, bring forth. If no useful seeds are put into it, then an abundance of useless weed seeds will fall therein, and will continue to produce their kind. Just as a gardener cultivates his plot, keeping it free from weeds, and growing the flowers and fruits which he requires, so may a man tend the garden of his mind, weeding out all the wrong, useless, and impure thoughts, and cultivating toward perfection the flowers and fruits of right, useful, and pure thoughts, By pursuing this process, a man sooner or later discovers that he is the master gardener of his soul, the director of his life." ~James Allen

It doesn't matter who you are, what your religion is, where you live, what your age is… this law is true for every human being:

The Law of Attraction also known as, 'success-consciousness', 'power of thought', 'like attracts like' 'what goes around comes around', 'karma' or the 'Law of Magnetism' states that **all of our thoughts, all the images in our minds, and all the emotions/feelings connected with our thoughts will sooner or later manifest as our reality**. The law of 'cause and effect', 'sow and reap', the law of 'intention' also give us a similar message.

*image above has been taken from the book *"Your Life: A Practical Guide To Happiness, Peace and Fulfilment"*

Modern science has proved the law of attraction by the fundamentals of quantum physics. Ancient wisdom too consists of references which prove the above as true/fact. Every major religion has documented this in one form or other.

> *"What you resist, you attract, because you are powerfully focused on it with emotion. To change anything, go within and emit a new signal with your thoughts and feelings." ~Rhonda Byrne*

Taking responsibility of your life and knowing the fact that you attract people and events in life is scary, isn't it?

Most people focus on what they don't want so they attract more of it in their lives. We must focus on what we do want.

Are you now thinking that is it your thinking which matters? Yes, that is all that matters to start with. Repetitive thoughts become beliefs.

> *"Habits of thinking need not be forever. One of the most significant findings in psychology in the last twenty years is that individuals can choose the way they think." ~Dr. Martin Seligman*

Science is proving it now and the old spiritual books said it centuries ago that **negative thoughts are the primary source of all the internal and external diseases and illnesses!**

So feeding that 'evil' wolf isn't just making you feel bad emotionally, it can make you feel bad physically too. All the more reason to make your 'good' wolf stronger!

> *"There is too much negativity around. My health suffered due to this. Constant negativity does affect a person." ~Katrina Kaif Turcotte*
> (Celebrated Actress, Philanthropist, Inspiring Role Model, Wax figure at Madame Tussauds London, Ambassador for UN's Global Goals Campaign)

"The physical creation follows the mental, just as a building follows a blueprint. If you don't make a conscious effort to visualize who you are and what you want in life, then you empower other people and circumstances to shape you and your life by default." ~Dr. Stephen R. Covey

Explore Yourself

What thoughts do you regularly think that feed your 'evil' wolf?

What thoughts could you think instead that would feed your 'good' wolf?

How many times a day you have thoughts full of doubt, fear and uncertainty? Keep a log for a week.

The inner speech, your thoughts, can cause you to be rich or poor, loved or unloved, happy or unhappy, attractive or unattractive, powerful or weak.
~Ralph Charell

The Voice in Your Head

How you talk to yourself determines how you feel about yourself, and determines the actions you take.

All of us, all the time, talk to ourselves. We have a voice inside our head which we call 'self-talk' (also known as internal dialogue, self-suggestions, inner-critique etc.). It may be loud or silent and includes our conscious thoughts but the majority of it is our unconscious beliefs or assumptions.

It says things like – should I go to work today?; I'm hungry; I wonder what my kid is doing right now; wow that girl is attractive; I really like those shoes; oh I have a headache; maybe I should go to the shop later; I hope...; If only...; I wish...; What will they...; I am...; I can't...; Why me... I may... etc.

'I shouldn't have eaten that much! I'm so stupid. I'll never lose the weight to get into a swimsuit. I don't like myself in the mirror!'

I have a bad memory! I just know it won't work! I will never have any savings! I ain't good enough for this! My desk is always a mess! There is no way I can handle this! I can't say 'no' to people! I can't take it anymore! If only I had more time! S/he drives me mad! I hate my job! If only I had more money! I am unlucky! I am never organised! If only I had that degree! I am depressed!

Do YOU think things like this? These kind of thoughts or feelings are called negative self-talk (also known as self-defeating, self-blame, scarcity mindset, self-doubt). If someone else shouted at you with all the blames above, how would you react? Would it feel good? If someone said the above for your child, would you believe it?

Then WHY do you take this crap from yourself, from your own negative voice?

Another thing which is common is that many times the voice in our head isn't ours. It could be one of our parents, teachers, authority figures, partner, close friend or colleague... someone whose feedback/blame really mattered at the time we created that belief.

"Like food is to the body, self-talk is to the mind. Don't let any junk thoughts repeat in your head." ~Maddy Malhotra

Well known psychologist, anxiety treatment specialist and author, Edmund J. Bourne, Ph.D, states that self-talk is so automatic and subtle you don't notice it or the effect it has on your moods and feelings. Anxious self-talk is typically irrational but almost always sounds like the truth. Negative self-talk perpetuates avoidance and can initiate or aggravate a panic attack.

In many situations, the only thing you can control is your own response. Changing self-talk from negative to positive is an excellent way to manage that response (rather than reacting badly with anger or snapping).

"Every waking moment we talk to ourselves about the things we experience. Our self talk, the thoughts we communicate to ourselves, in turn controls the way we feel and act." ~John Lembo

Most of us are unaware of the words we use on a regular basis. We weren't taught that the **words we regularly use to describe our experiences and conditions in life impact and influence our emotional states.** So unknowingly we make our states worse by using and relating high-intensity bad or negative words to our experiences in life. For example using the word 'depressed' for feeling 'down' or 'frustrated'.

You can use words to change how you think, which will change your feelings, decisions and results. Wisely selecting the words we use to describe the experiences in and of our lives can make us feel better thus impacting our decisions and actions. Don't limit your emotional joy with your disabling words! Use the words 'very good' or 'excellent' rather than feeling 'better'.

Research shows that people who make *generic* explanations for their failures give up on everything when failure strikes in one area of their lives however those who make *specific* explanations may become helpless in that one part of their lives, yet continue to achieve in other areas. For example using:

I am repulsive to her Vs. I am repulsive

You haven't talked to me lately Vs. You don't talk to me

Diet plans never work when I eat out Vs. Diets never work

My wife is stressed when there is a lot of housework to do Vs. My wife is always stressed

"As human beings, we continually tell ourselves stories of success or failure; of power or victimhood; stories that endure for an hour, or a day, or an entire lifetime. We have stories about our work, our families and relationships, our health; about what we want and what we're capable of achieving. Yet, while our stories profoundly affect how others see us and we see ourselves, too few of us even recognize that we're telling stories, or what they are, or that we can change them and, in turn, transform our very destinies." ~Jim Loehr

Our questions determine our thoughts. The questions we ask ourselves, in our head, determine where we focus, how we think, how we feel, and what we decide and/or do. Most people ask ineffective questions of themselves which trigger lame or negative thoughts and negatively affect their results.

These types of questions turn our focus away from what we want and trigger thoughts of what we don't want. They are disempowering and keep us focused on our problems, failures and shortcomings. Basically they bring up things which remind us of what is wrong and what isn't working in our lives.

Effective questions are empowering. They turn our focus to what we want and usually trigger solution oriented thoughts.

For example:

Ineffective questions: Why can't I be happy? How come I never have time for myself? Why do I often feel down?

Effective questions: What can I do to uplift myself? What can I read, listen or watch that would inspire me? Who can I talk to? What places can I visit? Are these feelings a call for change in life? Are there any physical exercises or meditation techniques I can do to feel better?

"I am the greatest; I said that even before I knew I was."
~Muhammad Ali

"The most influential and frequent voice you hear is your inner-voice. It can work in your favour or against you, depending on what you listen to and act upon." ~Maddy Malhotra

Explore Yourself

Have you noticed that most of us use extreme words for negative experiences but average words for describing positive experiences, feelings or results?

How many times do you engage in self-criticism versus self-praise in your mind and while talking about yourself with others?

How many times do you complain/blame/moan versus appreciate/praise/thank?

What is your internal battle about? Is it holding you back from moving forward in life?

Ask yourself: in which areas of my life I cannot achieve my goals with the story I believe and repeat?

Now, create new positive stories which would take you where you want to go in every area of your life and start believing them even though the old ones would try to take over! (remember Your Beliefs/Values Affect Your Stories so change your beliefs first)

YOUR NOTES

YOUR NOTES

People spend a lifetime searching for happiness; looking for peace. They chase idle dreams, addictions, religions, even other people, hoping to fill the emptiness that plagues them. The irony is the only place they ever needed to search was within.

~R. L. Anderson

Emotions - What Are They Making You Do?

Most of us experience far more negative emotions, everyday, than positive ones.

In chapter 2 we discussed that the levels of happiness have dropped significantly and it has become an occasional thing! **It is very important to know that we are emotional creatures. All that we do is to fulfil some emotional need.**

The limbic system (or Paleomammalian brain) supports functions including emotion and behaviour but it doesn't understand language. What that means is that the part of your brain which is responsible for your behaviour doesn't understand language, it understands feelings!

Deficiency of vitamins, vital minerals and nutrients can be taken care of with supplements and diet, but what about the deficiency of self-love, self-praise, self-respect? What do you do for the needs like fulfilment, peace of mind or inner-joy? Negative emotions lead to many mental health problems and many physical illnesses.

"To experience positive/healthy emotions you don't need a big house or a nice car or a managerial job or a million dollar in your bank."
~Maddy Malhotra

Society today is material and fame oriented. We aren't taught that it's the internal-world which matters more than the external; that it's the feelings and emotions which are the fuel of human beings.

The people who themselves didn't know much about creating a high quality life, programmed you to see the world wrong way round. Most of us are concerned about what other people see us as, the clothes we wear, our professional designation, our financial status, the house we live in, the car we drive, the school our kids go to etc.

BUT the truth is that we are 'emotional' creatures. Every action of ours is influenced by our emotions. All that we do for others and for our social image is far less important than experiencing inner-happiness, peace, love and gratitude.

Intellect is not a substitute for emotions. We are conditioned to live for others, to live by the rules of the society which is driven by money, fame and fears!

Negative emotions have a purpose too. They tell you something isn't right and must be looked in to.

"Fear and pain should be treated as signals not to close our eyes but to open them wider." ~Dr. Nathaniel Branden

"We often try to hide the emotion or run from it. Emotions play a fundamental role in life. They help us to form relationships, experience growth, and evaluate our performance. Besides that, they prompt us to learn and sometimes prompt us to quit, fight, cry, lie, and/or to hide."
~Dr. Erik Fisher

It's the emotional issues which people can't handle and they use all sorts of means such as stimulants, self-harm or comfort eating as a solution or distraction.

We have many emotional needs like love, certainty, fulfilment, variety and significance. A part of these needs can be fulfilled by ourselves, however these days most of us try to fulfil these needs completely from outside, hence we become stuck in a loop of showing-off, pleasing others, approval addiction, changing sex partners etc. because most of us have a low self-esteem. Yes we do need some approval or attention from others but a lot of it can come from within us. This is why the fear of rejection is one of the most common in us today! We are begging for love and approval from others. Explained in detail in the self-esteem chapter.

This type of society, which is full of people with negative/limiting beliefs about themselves, is bound to have more and more mental health patients! Studies show that positive emotions reduce the negative effects of stress on the body (physiology) and improve problem solving skills (decisions leading to results).

"At the end of the day it's not 'what looks good' that matters, it's 'what feels' good." ~Maddy Malhotra

Every one of us has the choice: to take personal offence from another person's behavior or not.

It is said that on an occasion when the Buddha was teaching a group of people, he found himself on the receiving end of a fierce outburst of abuse from a bystander, who was for some reason very angry.

The Buddha listened patiently while the stranger vented his rage, and then the Buddha said to the group and to the stranger, "If someone gives a gift to another person, who then chooses to decline it, tell me, who would then own the gift? The giver, or the person who refuses to accept the gift?"

"The giver," said the group after a little thought. "Any fool can see that," added the angry stranger.

"Then it follows, does it not," said the Buddha, "Whenever a person tries to abuse us, or to unload their anger on us, we can each choose to decline or to accept the abuse; whether to make it ours or not. By our personal response to the abuse from another, we can choose who owns and keeps the bad feelings."

"The primary cause of unhappiness is never the situation but thoughts about it. Be aware of the thoughts you are thinking. Separate them from the situation, which is always neutral. It is as it is." ~Eckhart Tolle

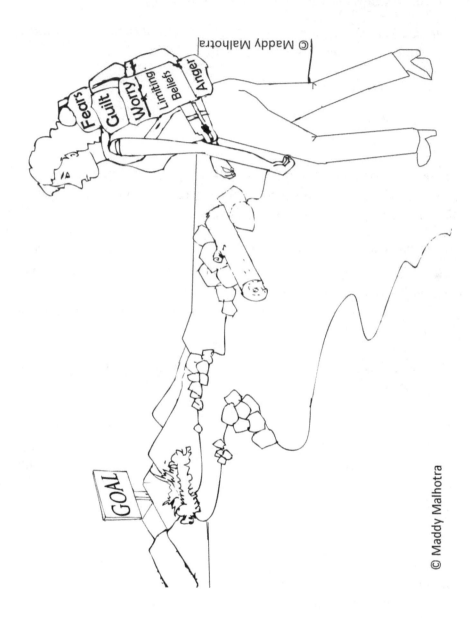

If you continue to carry **emotional baggage** from the past then how would you move ahead, with the speed you desire, to achieve your goals? It usually holds us back and kills our happiness, peace and esteem!

Research has proven that negative emotions such as stress, anxiety, fear, lack of forgiveness, anger, envy, depression etc. can cause the release of chemicals (neuro-peptides) by the brain that in turn create poor health in the body. Symptoms such as poor digestion, irregular heartbeat, high blood pressure and inflammation of the body parts, ulcers, pains, skin diseases, IBS, and panic attacks are all traceable to stress on the body caused by excess and uncontrolled negative emotions. Illnesses such as cancer, heart diseases, diabetes and depression can also be linked to unresolved negative emotions.

The field of *PsychoNeuroImmunology* suggests significant effects of negative emotions on our immune system. Hormones such as adrenaline and cortisol (helpful when required) are released in unexpected amounts when a person experiences negative emotions. Such chemicals weaken the immune system. They become toxic for our body and can cause our bodies to create toxic cells which cause disease. On the other hand, positive emotions such as joy, happiness, fulfillment, contentment etc. can make the brain release chemicals which can strengthen the immune system and help an individual to prevent and/or heal cancer, and other illnesses.

Isn't it surprising that we can, by controlling our thoughts, prevent diseases and heal our bodies? The belief that the state of our mind affects the health of our body is not just a recent invention. It has been emphasized and repeated in every major religious book (as far as 5000 years ago) and by many self-realized people till date.

Explore Yourself

When you experience a negative emotion ask: What can I learn from this feeling? Is there something I must resolve?

When someone behaves badly, how would you like to respond? Repeat your response to condition your mind.

When your thoughts/self-talk is based on the limiting or negative beliefs you hold then what kind of emotions do you experience?

YOUR NOTES

*Too many of us are not
living our dreams because
we are living our fears.*
~Les Brown

Get Rid Of Your Fears

Fear is the enemy of success. It holds you back from using your full potential and keeps you negative, frustrated and/or unhappy. It makes us mediocre!

We all have fears. Even the most successful people have fears to overcome. There is an endless list of things to be afraid of but an interesting part is that **successful and unsuccessful people all have the same fears!**

And what makes a big difference in our lives is how we respond to our fears and what we do to get rid of them, i.e. re-program our minds and stay committed to overcome our fear(s).

"The greatest mistake you can make in life is to continually fear you will make one." ~E Hubbard

Fears are beliefs which could have been created by our own experience or were, unconsciously, learned from others. For example, a client of mine learned the fear of spiders from her mother and another client learned the fear of becoming self-employed and the fear of investing money after observing his father's multiple failures. One of the biggest fears which hold us back is **the fear of the unknown.**

"You can conquer almost any fear if you will only make up your mind to do so. For remember, fear doesn't exist anywhere except in the mind." ~Dale Carnegie

Difference between Fear and Prudence

Most fears are irrational. For example, you might be afraid to make an important call because of the perceived fear of failure, or you might be afraid to face a colleague/partner who is a bully, or to start your own business (or change jobs) because you aren't sure whether you have the skills, confidence or charisma. It's these unreasonable fears that hold us back and keep us from becoming more successful or happier in our lives, they negatively affect our self-esteem and inner peace!

However there are other kinds of fear that are actually prudence. For example, you might be afraid of snakes or driving aggressively. Make sure you aren't pretending to be prudent by avoiding taking reasonable risks or by not stepping out of your comfort zone.

> *"Courage is not the absence of fear, but rather the judgment that something else is more important than fear."* ~Ambrose Redmoon

Whether you are afraid of something tangible, like spiders or heights or the fear of success, failure, loss, change or something else, you will have to do the following to take control of your life:

Acknowledge it - it's easy to deny or ignore your fears, even to yourself, in a society that emphasizes being brave and perfect. By owning it you take the first step towards taking control.

Write it down. Keep a journal to track your progress.

Analyse it - you need to understand your fear, so write down:

When did it begin? Is there a negative experience attached to it? Did you learn it from someone's reaction or experience? By exploring the deep beliefs behind your fears, you can transform your life for good.

How long have you been affected by this fear? What triggers it? Is it something obvious or tangible? Or do you need to be conscious the next time it happens and analyse it there and then? Find out everything that triggers it. How does it affect you? Write down how it influences different areas of your life? Figure out exactly what power it has over your emotions, attitude, decisions and behavior.

Visualise the desired outcome - after you identify and completely understand your fear, think about exactly what you would like to change. As discussed in the goals chapter, successful people imagine/visualise the outcome before they achieve results in reality. Be mentally prepared to deal with failure. Confronting a fear could be challenging, and you may have to confront your fear(s) many times before it's affect is gone from your life.

Set Goals – you may set small goals to help you overcome. Take little steps/actions to increase your confidence and slowly re-condition your mind with references of success. Celebrate each little achievement towards your goal. Appreciate yourself and affirm to succeed. Read the goals chapter to learn the best techniques.

Seek professional help – NLP or CBT practitioners may be able to assist you to get rid of fear(s), once you have had your session(s) with them you may find it easier to stay positive and accept the new beliefs/rules. Your fear may come back if you start repeating old negative thoughts! Remember, your beliefs control your attitude and decisions.

Fear can be used as a means to help us identify problems. Use the above steps to resolve them effectively. If what you fear is outside of your control (like economic crisis), write down a plan to adapt to it and change your business, career, spending or investment strategies accordingly.

Research shows that most people value 'security' over almost everything else in their lives. They put up with jobs they hate, unhealthy habits and miserable relationships in order to feel secure. To overcome fear(s), you must consciously replace 'security' with 'courage' as the thing you value most. You must decide, after recognising the negative effects of fear(s), that it's very important for you to have the courage to do what you must to succeed, rather than staying in your comfort/fearful zone and living in misery.

"Inaction breeds doubt and fear. Action breeds confidence and courage. If you want to conquer fear, do not sit home and think about it. Go out and get busy." ~Dale Carnegie

It takes lots of determination and energy to deal with fear. When you encounter setbacks you may feel like giving up. Your limiting self-beliefs may try to stop you too, but you must persevere even when it seems impossible. Visualise how you would feel and what you would achieve once you have conquered your fear(s). Don't leave it up to fate. Don't be hard on yourself if you have multiple fears, just deal with them one at a time. Don't let other people hold you back. Be aware when someone is feeding your fears (bad wolf) by underestimating your ability or by scaring you of the consequences. Surround yourself with genuine well-wishers who support you reaching your full potential.

There is no substitute in life to taking action. Action is the true way to learn. Failure is inevitable, so follow the old saying: fall down 5 times get back up 6. When you learned how to walk or to ride a bike, did you get it the first time, of course not. You tried again and again until you were successful.

"Fear is never a reason for quitting; it is only an excuse."
~Norman Vincent Peale

I have learned that it's the actions that scared me most of the time (leaving a high paying corporate job to self employment, migrating to the UK), but they have also paid off the most. That doesn't mean these moves weren't hard, but I managed to re-condition my brain to overcome the momentary fear and step up with faith.

You can't be successful if you're ruled by fear.

*do not attempt anything dangerous by yourself or do anything against the law

"What is needed, rather than running away or controlling or suppressing or any other resistance, is understanding fear; that means, watch it, learn about it, and come directly into contact with it. We are to learn about fear, not how to escape from it." ~J Krishnamurti

Explore Yourself

I mean now. Not tomorrow; not next week. Right now, before you read the next chapter - Call that person. Write that email. Create a business plan. Take a step now!

YOUR NOTES

How Life Works

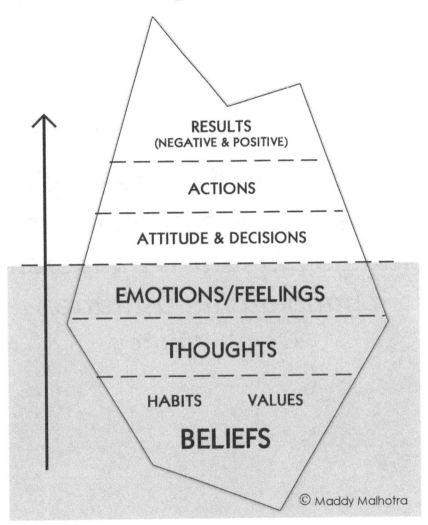

RESULTS
(NEGATIVE & POSITIVE)

ACTIONS

ATTITUDE & DECISIONS

EMOTIONS/FEELINGS

THOUGHTS

HABITS   VALUES

BELIEFS

© Maddy Malhotra

The greatest discovery of all time is that a person can change his future by merely changing his attitude.
~Oprah Winfrey

Create a Positive Attitude

Your attitude can make or break almost any situation. You can have a positive attitude about the events in your life, or you can complain, blame and be miserable. You decide. A positive attitude is a choice you make in almost any circumstance.

People with negative attitudes are the perpetual victims in life and they are unpleasant to be around. They focus their thoughts and energy on their negative pasts and negative present hence they create a negative future for themselves (as explained in the thoughts chapter).

People who are controlled by their attitudes tend to be pessimistic and fearful. They simply allow themselves to get stuck in their own little miserable world.

The main cause of negative attitude can be low self-esteem, anger, resentment, stress, inability to handle change or merely seeking attention.

"Happiness doesn't depend on any external conditions, it is governed by our mental attitude." ~Dale Carnegie

Life is full of surprises and believe me challenges (problems) will always be there. On the other side human beings can't be perfect hence we can't be positive all the time however we can change our attitude at will.

Your attitude transforms into actions. You need to understand the difference between 'Respond' and 'Reaction'. What do you do when you meet challenges or difficult people? To be a responsive individual you need to condition your mind by affirming your response to situations and people.

I agree that life is 10% what happens to me and 90% how I react. **We are in charge of our attitudes**.

Sadly, luck and talent are overrated and Attitude is underrated these days!

Start by becoming aware of your attitude in various situations. Once you have identified which situations or people influence your attitude then start programming your mind to stay in control.

"We cannot change our past. We can not change the fact that people act in a certain way. We can not change the inevitable. The only thing we can do is play on the one string we have, and that is our attitude."
~Charles R. Swindoll

Explore Yourself

Do you have an attitude of gratitude or you are one of many who keep moaning, blaming and whining about life and other people?

How well do you handle stress?

Are you conscious of your attitude at work and/or home?

Do you look for solutions for the challenges (problems) in life?

Are you controlled by your attitude OR

Are you in control of your attitude?

Which are your harmful/unhealthy attitudes?

YOUR NOTES

We are what we repeatedly do. Excellence, then, is not an act, but a habit.
~Aristotle

Developing Good Habits

Most of our lives are habitual. You do the same things you did yesterday, the day before and every day for the last month. Habits, good or bad, make you who you are. The key is being able to control them. Little changes that, when put on autopilot, can result in an improved quality of life.

"First we make our habits, then our habits make us."
~Charles C. Noble

A Habit usually takes up to 28 days to change. It's sufficient to condition or recondition your subconscious mind. It will be easier and get you better results if your focus on changing one habit at a time. Four weeks may seem like a long time to focus on only one change, but I've found trying to change more than 2-3 habits at a time to be 'out of control'.

However, if a habit is giving you a lot of pain, it can be deleted or replaced in a matter of hours depending on your commitment and intensity of negative results you are experiencing. After learning the long term consequences of not consuming fibre I changed the type of cereals and food, I ate, within a day. It really depends on how quickly you can replace the need, and condition your mind for the change.

A very important thing to do is to replace your lost need(s). You can't just delete habits without replacing the needs they fulfil otherwise you will adopt the unwanted habit(s) again! Giving up television might mean you need to find a new way to relax, deal with negative emotions and thoughts or how you retain information. You will have to fill the void with something, healthier or positive, which satisfies your needs. This is the reason why the majority of people who, by using will power alone, try to quit smoking or stop eating unhealthy food can't resist temptation for long! This is why it is of paramount importance that you should <u>replace</u> those old negative habits with new, refreshing and positive ideals.

79

"Fear is a habit, so is self-pity, defeat, anxiety, despair, hopelessness and resignation. You can eliminate all of these negative habits with two simple resolves, 'I can and I will'." ~Napoleon Hill

Use the techniques, discussed in the goal setting chapter, to disregard your bad habits and to create good ones. Focus on positive results not on seeking instant gratification, which you obtain from old habits. **Use affirmations to focus on what you want and what you will achieve** (rather than fears, doubts or excuses).

Make it a fun-filled process, be creative and find ways to leverage for example give a friend or colleague $100 and ask him or her to return it to you only when you have changed the unwanted habit. Make sure you appreciate and reward yourself.

If your change creates more pain in your life than joy, it is going to be hard to stick to. When the going gets tough remind yourself of the positive consequences, feelings, effects on your life and on the life of people you care about. Don't go to the gym if you hate it instead find diets and/or exercises that are fun to follow and support you.

Remember, consistency is the key. Be confident and make sure your desired habit is consistent and is repeated every day for four weeks or more. It will re-wire your neurons and become permanent in your mind.

Like many things in life, you can't know whether a new habit will work until you try it.

"Habit is the intersection of knowledge (what to do), skill (how to do), and desire (want to do)." ~Stephen R. Covey

"World-class habits create world-class results. Poor habits kill. If you want to succeed, focus as much on your habits as you do on your goal." ~Steve Siebold

Which habits are unhealthy for your mind, body, relationships or success?

Which new habits would you replace these with?

Which habits can you create to increase relaxation, love and happiness in your daily life?
(I have a habit of watching at least 15 minutes of comedy twice a day)
Come up with some creative ideas and implement.

Personal leadership is the process of keeping your vision and values before you and aligning your life to be congruent with them.
~Dr. Stephen Covey

The Driving Force behind Your Decisions

If I were to ask you "what are your values"? Can you easily list them?

If you have some difficulty listing your values then you are not aware of your personal compass hence the lack of fulfillment in your life!

"Like beliefs, in most cases, we don't create our values... others do."
~Maddy Malhotra

Successful people are consciously (or unconsciously) aware of their values i.e. the things that are important to them. Values can be all shapes and sizes for example love, contribution to society, honesty, personal growth, joy, adventure, health, wealth etc.

I believe that we all have core values; whether we recognize them or not. When these values are compromised we tend to feel bad and when we live our lives in-line with our values we tend to feel more fulfilled and in control. We all have secondary/goal specific values too. These values are appropriate for a certain amount of time until we achieve desired results and then something else takes priority in life for which we change the priority levels of our values. This continues forever. For example; you may want to reduce 'weight' before your wedding or you may want to promote your value of 'family/love' when you have a new born or you want to prioritise 'learning' before you apply for a new job.

Unfortunately, most of us don't have a clear idea of what's important to us.

Values decide our direction in life and these ideals and values can stem from our parents, teachers, authority figures, super heroes, religion, sports stars or other influential personalities.

From our beliefs we derive our values, which can either be beneficial or damaging when compared with evidence in our lives, but nonetheless hold true for us.

Once your core values are realised, you will gain a valuable understanding of just who you are and what makes you tick. You will begin to resolve the hidden conflicts in your life and decrease stress. Your decisions become aligned with your own values (not with someone else's).

Our beliefs and values can differ over time as we encounter evidence or have experiences that challenge our previously held rules. On the other hand our beliefs and values can also strengthen (reinforced) by experience or evidence.

The difference in values is a big reason behind conflicts in relationships for example the top 3 values of a man could be finances, security and comfort whereas a woman may have family, love, health which means the decisions would vary and the amount of time, money and energy spent would be in completely different areas of life.

"Be more concerned with your character than your reputation, because your character is what you really are, while your reputation is merely what others think you are." ~John Wooden

What is truly important to you in life?

Brainstorm a list of your values. Try to reduce your responses to a single word or two that summarizes each value. You might end up with a list like this:

- Love
- Health
- Wealth
- Happiness
- Fun/Adventure
- Comfort
- Success/Personal Growth
- Learning
- Peace
- Intimacy
- Security
- Family/Relationships

Now ask yourself:

Why *xyz* value is high on my list?

Is it derived from the beliefs created by me or programmed by others?

Would re-eliciting/arranging my values give me true happiness and fulfilment?

Which new values would be useful for me at this time in my life (depending on your short and long term goals)?

YOUR NOTES

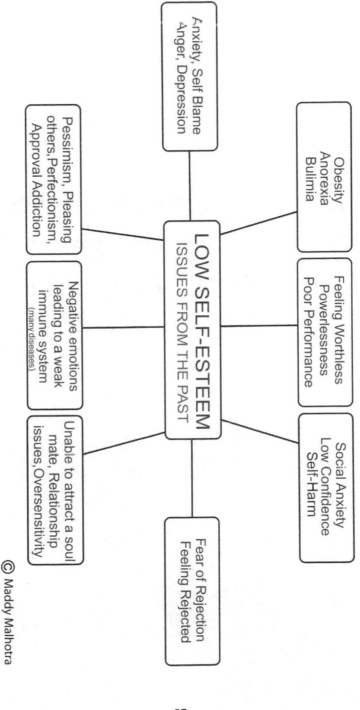

LOW SELF-ESTEEM
ISSUES FROM THE PAST

Anxiety, Self Blame
Anger, Depression

Obesity
Anorexia
Bulimia

Feeling Worthless
Powerlessness
Poor Performance

Social Anxiety
Low Confidence
Self-Harm

Fear of Rejection
Feeling Rejected

Unable to attract a soul
mate, Relationship
issues, Oversensitivity

Negative emotions
leading to a weak
immune system
(many diseases)

Pessimism, Pleasing
others, Perfectionism,
Approval Addiction

© Maddy Malhotra

87

Low self-esteem is like driving through life with your hand-break on.
~Maxwell Maltz

Secrets to High Self Esteem

Mirrors don't reflect it, but it's there when we look at ourselves. It affects how we feel, but we can't touch it. It influences our self-talk and what we say about ourselves to others, but we can't hear it. It controls our attitudes and behaviour, but we aren't unaware of it.

What is this powerful, yet mysterious factor? It's our **self-esteem**!

I am not good enough.

I am fat.

I am unlovable.

I am stupid.

I am not important.

I am ugly.

I am inferior.

I am bad.

I am a mess inside.

I will never get anywhere in life.

I can't…

I am a failure.

I will never…

"We have to learn to be our own best friends because we fall too easily into the trap of being our own worst enemies." ~Roderick Thorp

Self-esteem, the feeling of liking and respecting one's self, is the founding principle of success and happiness. Most psychologists agree that self-esteem is the critical determinant of a healthy personality. When you like and respect yourself, you always behave and perform better than if you did not. The more you like/love yourself, the more confidence you will have. Hence, the more efficient and effective you are in each area of your life. Self-esteem is the key to peak performance. So, whether it's your relationships, career and business or emotional and physical health, you must work on your self-esteem in order to perform at your best.

A lot of people live their lives imprisoned in the past or in the expectations of others. They never really try to break the boundaries that they or others created/set for them. Hence, they have limiting beliefs about what is possible for them.

Since childhood, we are told what to do and what is right or wrong. Our parents, teachers and handlers, by using carrots and sticks, wanted us to be and act in a certain way! As kids, we think they are right and adapt our behaviours in order to receive their attention, love and rewards. Unfortunately, most of us are still in the prison!

During childhood, we experience rejection, punishment, neglect, abuse, crticism, discrimination/favouritism/comparison, lack of praise, lack of touch and lack of love, and we may have been given labels, like bad, short, fat, idiot, naughty, etc. This is when we create negative and limiting beliefs/rules about our worth, appearance, abilities and who we are at our core.

"I am convinced all of humanity is born with more gifts than we know.
Most are born geniuses and just get de-geniused rapidly."
~Buckminster Fuller

As discussed in the beliefs chapter, **our negative beliefs about ourselves are opinions, not facts.**

Most of us suffer with one of the <u>biggest fears</u>: **the fear of being judged** and from the <u>most damaging belief</u>: **I am not good enough.**

For many of us, the **fear of rejection** is so dominating that we punish ourselves as a way to avoid the punishment from others. We humiliate ourselves or deny our desires and worth. We feel powerless and resentful.

I am bad at everything.

How stupid I am?

I never do it right.

Maybe if I reject myself, it won't hurt as bad when they reject me. We play a game that we can't win! It consumes us. We don't live our lives all because of the fears and limiting beliefs we have.

> *"It doesn't matter if thousands of people believe in you, unless You believe in You." ~Maddy Malhotra*

The majority of us suffer with the **addiction of seeking the approval** of others. We do realise that we are not children anymore, but we still want people to approve. Self-talk may sound like:

Am I doing it right?

Do I look right?

Am I behaving correctly?

Am I _____ right?

Are they all looking at me?

I hope they don't think I am a bad person.

I hope they like my...

The more close/important someone is in our life, the greater the need we feel to get them to approve. Our beliefs, thoughts and feelings, to a certain extent, revolve around the approval we crave. Hence, a lot of our choices and decisions are based on what they will think of us or how they will react.

There is nothing wrong with outside validation. For example, appreciation for your achievements, your paycheck or compliments for your good qualities are always welcome.

The problem comes in when you seek outside validation/approval as a source of self-esteem.

We all need esteem because it's a psychological need, but if you don't know where self-esteem comes from, if you don't know how to find it within yourself, you will be forced to seek false esteem from others, which is a never-ending unhealthy loop!

Often, we don't even get to the point of seeking true esteem because we're so afraid of the pain of self-exploration or the discomfort of changing ourselves by going against our existing self-beliefs. Therefore, we give up on (or never try) finding the true and healthier source of self-esteem and completely rely on the outside approval/validation. We use the worldly success as a source of esteem:

Look at my car.

Look at my house.

Look at my degrees.

My bank balance... my shoes... my hair style... my tattoos... my clothes... my figure/muscles... my luxury items... my spouse... The list goes on, but what if you lose your job? What if you and your partner don't get along? What if you make a loss on your investment? What if your elegant car gets wrecked?

What's going to happen to your esteem? What type of emotions would you experience?

Please understand that outside approval/validation is required, but it should *not* be a source of your esteem.

A very important thing to remember is that having lots of money/materials, an ideal body shape or being religious does *not* guarantee a high self-esteem. Your image is in your mind. How you see yourself depends on the rules you use to judge yourself (i.e. the beliefs you have in mind, which determine whether a person is good, bad, fit, happy, successful, etc.)

"I am a human being, not a human doing. Don't equate your self-worth with how well you do things in life. You aren't what you do. If you are what you do, then when you don't...you aren't." ~Dr. Wayne Dyer

When our self-esteem is low, we have a **biased perception** of ourselves. We tend to notice things that are consistent with the negative/limiting beliefs we have about ourselves. We easily notice our shortcomings, weaknesses, flaws or anything we are unhappy about, but we disregard our qualities, skills, strengths and other good things about ourselves! Our focus is usually on what we do wrong, our imperfect physical appearance or negative predictions for our future.

Similarly, we interpret/judge things according to the rules we have about ourselves rather than what really is! We think/choose self-criticism rather than appreciation, encouragement or self-acceptance. Even when things go well, our low self-esteem can diminish pleasure in what we achieve and make us overlook or disqualify anything that doesn't fit within our negative rules about us.

For example, if Liz, a client of mine, was complimented with the words "you are looking good today," she used to think she looked bad up until now or thought others were being nice/kind, and she never believed/accepted the compliment(s) she received.

*"The strongest single factor in prosperity consciousness is self-esteem:
believing you can do it, believing you deserve it, believing you will get it"
~Jerry Gillies*

Are you a fortune-teller? A clairvoyant? If not, why **anticipate the
worst?**

We predict events will turn out in a negative way because our core
beliefs about ourselves are negative. And no matter how things turn
out, we are likely to put painful or negative labels on events. This
strengthens the negative beliefs we have about ourselves and makes us
more likely to forecast worse in the future!

Past does not equal the future, so why judge yourself by the results/rules from your performance in the past?

"Research has shown that low self-esteem (lasting negative beliefs about the self) may contribute towards a range of difficulties, including depression, suicidal thinking, eating disorders and social anxiety."
~Dr. Melanie Fennel

Self-critical thoughts and detrimental predictions have a huge impact on our mood/feelings, and as explained earlier, it affects our attitude, decisions and behaviour. They ensure our self-esteem stays low.

Everyone will think I'm an idiot if I...

People would laugh at me if I...

I won't be able to cope.

They will reject me if I...

Ask yourself: how do I feel and behave when I am hard on myself or I put myself down?

"We need to stop hating ourselves just because we are not someone else's idea of who we should be." ~Alicia Brooks

The day I started to love myself and started to feel proud of my achievements (big and small), I started to experience inner joy, and the negative chatter in my mind calmed down! It can take some time to re-condition your mind, but it is possible to create positive and healthy self-beliefs.

The more you love yourself, the more you will be able to receive/feel the love from other people in your life. Ask yourself: would a person who loves him/herself think and act like I do?

Unfortunately, we're taught to love others, not ourselves. We're told that self-love equates with selfishness and narcissism!

"You have been criticizing yourself for years and it hasn't worked. Try approving of yourself and see what happens." ~Louise Hay

You have two choices: either you wait for your luck or use the tools and techniques that have helped many individuals to design a different destiny. Consciously choose new self-beliefs, build self-esteem and align your attitude and behaviour accordingly.

You deserve happiness and peace of mind. Design and live the life that *you* desire. **The choice, as always, is yours.**

"In order to develop your confidence in yourself and your self-esteem, you will need to begin approaching situations that you have been avoiding. Otherwise, your life will continue to be restricted by your fears, and you will never gain the information you need to have a realistic, positive perspective on yourself." ~Dr. Melanie Fennel

"Intention of seeking attention is an addiction. A vicious cycle which damages your health, finances and relationships. It will NOT improve your self-image, increase your self-worth or fulfill the need of genuine praise." ~Maddy Malhotra

*narcissism, arrogance, big-ego and selfishness are unhealthy!

Analysing your negative beliefs and thoughts may sound scary and you may want to avoid them but if you want to reduce/stop self-criticism effectively, it is necessary to look them straight in the face. You need to take *responsibility* for it. When you think about 'responsibility' you must focus on the positive possibilities not the negative past events which make you feel guilty or blame yourself and others.

Do I love myself? Is my self-esteem high?

If not, then why?

Am I lovable? Does anyone love me?

If not, then why?

Am I a perfectionist? If Yes, then why?

Am I addicted to the approval of others?

If Yes, then why?

Will I ever be able to - respect myself/believe in myself/heal from the trauma/speak in public?

If not, then why?

Write the beliefs you learned about yourself, during the first 18 years of your life, from your:

1. Father

2. Mother

3. Siblings

4. Friends

5. Teachers

6. Others

Which of these beliefs continue to dominate your thoughts today?

For your <u>self</u>, write down the beliefs which aren't serving you. Then for each problem and related beliefs ask yourself – How did this specific belief impact various areas of my life? Why is this belief still in operation? Which beliefs would serve me better? Write the beliefs you would like to replace the old ones with.

For each negative rule/belief you identify, ask yourself:

What is it costing me emotionally, financially and affecting my relationships (list the pains)?

Do you easily accept compliments/praise?

Think about your reactions when things go wrong or do not work out as planned. What type of thoughts run through your mind? Are you hard on yourself? Do you put yourself down? Do you call yourself names?

Think - what do words like - Weak Ugly Fat Unlikeable Unwanted Stupid Worthless Inferior Inadequate Useless Stupid Incompetent – do to your motivation, confidence, mood/feelings, attitude and behavior?

What affirmations (refer to the goal setting chapter) can you create which can replace the negative self-talk you do about yourself? (start seeing the good things/points in your actions, behavior and appearance. And remember, perfectionism isn't healthy and can be destructive in long-term)

Real examples from my coaching clients' experiences -

When the inner-gremlin tries to discount compliments:

She said I am looking good today. It means I used to look bad up till now or was she just being nice to me.

Tell that voice not to assume and be positive:

I did make an effort to get ready today so I may be looking well. She is a well wisher so why would she lie? People have complimented, for my looks, in the past too. I can and do look good when..

If the evil wolf is unrealistically generalizing:

I got a D in the exam. I don't understand anything in this class. I'm such an idiot. I shouldn't be in college.

Tell that voice something specific:

I didn't perform well in this one exam, but I've done O.K. on all the projects/homework. There are some things which I don't understand, but I can make an effort and seek help in order to perform better next time.

When the inner-voice is unsympathetic:

"People said they liked my presentation, but it wasn't as good as it should have been. Can't believe no-one noticed the errors I made."

Counteract by being reassuring:

"Wow, they liked it! It wasn't perfect, but I worked hard on it and did a good job. I'm proud of myself for creating and delivering it successfully."

YOUR NOTES

YOUR NOTES

YOUR NOTES

YOUR NOTES

Many people fail in life, not for lack of ability or brains or even courage but simply because they have never organized their energies around a goal.
~Elbert Hubbard

Effective Goal Setting

Setting goals without changing your self talk and beliefs will not work in the long term. Remember, most of us sabotage our success because of our beliefs, fears and assumptions. Also, our subconscious mind keeps us away from pain hence it stops us from taking actions which are outside our comfort zone. We must reprogram it to move forward or to take risk or to be uncomfortable.

Assess where you are in life right now and where you want to go. When you focus on something you achieve it, whether the goal is personal or professional. Applied focus is immeasurably beneficial yet so hard for most people. Don't leave commitments in your brain. Note them on paper or computer or mobile phone. This will create clarity and keep you committed since it is easy to dismiss a thought, but harder to reject a promise printed in front of you.

"The key to success is to focus our conscious mind on things we desire not things we fear." ~Brian Tracy

There are many models for goal setting and the most commonly used is The S.M.A.R.T. model which states that your goals must be **S**pecific, **M**easurable, **A**chievable, **R**ealistic and **T**imed

Which I agree with BUT **these 5 aren't enough!**

We are emotional creatures, we think in pictures and we talk to ourselves hence I had to create something which when added to the SMART goals will inspire and motivate you to achieve goals and will increase the chance of you taking action.

"I would die without goals or a focus. I need something to keep me going." ~Katrina Kaif Turcotte
(Celebrated Actress, Philanthropist, Inspiring Role Model, Wax figure at Madame Tussauds London, Ambassador for UN's Global Goals Campaign)

The **EVA**™ model

E - In the previous chapters we have learned that emotions are responsible for our decisions and actions. Emotions create motion. Is your goal emotionally charged? <u>The stronger the attached emotions, the more motivated you will be to achieve your goal.</u> Ask yourself: How will I feel when I will achieve this goal? What emotional gain or pleasure this goal will bring me? List as many as possible.

V - A vision board or a creativity collage is typically a poster board on which you paste images of things, people, money and success you desire. It represents what you would like to be, have and do once you have achieved your goals. You can write the feelings, with each picture, that you will experience when you have achieved your goals.

Go to: **www.coachmaddy.com/visionboard** to see one!

"Formulate and stamp indelibly on your mind a mental picture of yourself as succeeding. Hold this picture tenaciously. Your mind will seek to develop the picture. . . Do not build up obstacles in your imagination."
~Norman Vincent Peale

A – Affirmations are statements we speak, listen to and/or read for a desirable outcome. We know the power of repetitions. We can reprogram our mind i.e. overwrite the negative, limiting or false beliefs, by repeating positive words and phrases.

Create *affirmations* for all the goals you have created. The subconscious does not process the words 'don't' or 'not' (or differentiate between good and bad), so Always use positive words, State it in the present tense, make it very specific (facts/figures/levels/amount). It must show your subconscious mind a clear picture or direction. Add feelings where ever you can.

Listen to my affirmations at: **www.coachmaddy.com/affirmations**

Examples –

✓ I am a money magnet and/or money flows easily to me.
✓ I manage my money wisely and/or I invest my money wisely so that it multiplies.
✓ I eat nutritious and healthy food to keep my body functioning optimally.
✓ My fitness routine gives me the physical and emotional results I desire.
✓ My relationship with (*person/name*) is becoming more loving and committed.
✓ I am lovable. I am open to love. People love me.
✓ I value my time and use it wisely.
✓ I am creative, organised and resourceful at work.
✓ I choose to be happy.
✓ I believe in myself.
✓ I am grateful for ____

*initially your mind may not believe these affirmations but if you change your beliefs and take consistent action towards your goals, your mind will accept these and will focus on achieving.

Examples of EVA™ goals -

It is 1ˢᵗ June 2015, I am so proud of my achievements. My monthly income now is $10,000 and now I pay an extra $300 towards my loans. I have a savings account and I deposit $500 every month for holidays/kids/new car etc. I am in control of my finances. I manage money very well. I feel…

It is (date) and I feel (positive emotions) as I have now achieved my ideal size/weight. I eat (details of a healthy diet). I (details of physical exercise) everyday/times per week. I (benefits in other areas of life).

"Whatever you do, you need courage. Whatever course you decide upon, there is always someone to tell you that you are wrong. There are always difficulties arising that tempt you to believe your critics are right. To map out a course of action and follow it to an end requires some of the same courage that a soldier needs. Peace has its victories, but it takes brave men and women to win them." ~Ralph Waldo Emerson

And don't forget to reward yourself during and after achieving your goals. Make reward a part of your goal setting so you have more reasons to act upon.

Explore Yourself

What would happen if you didn't attain this goal? List all the consequences, pains, negative feelings etc. What will the impact of this be in the other areas of your life?

How often will you review your progress?

Who could support you in achieving this goal?

What additional skills and/or resources may be required to facilitate this goal?

What do you visualise? Your heart's desire or your fears.

How will you celebrate your successes? How would you reward yourself? Who else will be happy or proud for your achievements?

YOUR NOTES

This life is yours. Take the power to choose what you want to do and do it well. Take the power to love what you want in life and love it honestly. Take the power to control your own life. No one else can do it for you. Take the power to make your life happy. ~Susan Schutz

Take Action to Make it Happen

Now that you are aware of what is stopping you and you have changed some of those thoughts, beliefs and self talk, there are no more excuses to stay stuck in your lack of confidence, your financial struggle, be overweight, have bad relationships or whatever difficulty you are having in your life.

It's time to break free. Stop avoiding and start creating.

You deserve to be rich. You deserve to live a happy life. You deserve peace of mind. You deserve your respect. You deserve loving relationships. And YES, it's all possible.

"Knowing is not enough; we must apply. Willing is not enough; we must do." ~Johann Wolfgang von Goethe

Most of us know what we want BUT we don't do much about it! But that isn't you anymore is it? You know that there is NO quick fix for it; that the **power of change is within you and only you can make that change; that choice is always there and you have complete control over what you choose to think and do.**

Most people live in their own comfort zone and romanticise about living the life of their dreams. They want it quickly and easily… but ask any successful person and he or she will tell you that you have to get rid of those niggling fears and doubts, believe in yourself, learn the best way to achieve your goals and be disciplined to be successful and fulfilled.

Like anything or anyone else (athletes, business startups, university students, successful professionals, singers, movie stars) becoming rich, gaining confidence, losing weight or increasing happiness takes time (believe it or not happiness is the fastest state of mind you can achieve out of all of the above because *you* can control/change your mental state!)

"Do or do not, there is no try." ~Yoda

No one likes self-discipline, but everyone needs self-discipline. Self-discipline is more than self-control. It is a process of channeling your intentions, values, actions, and habits to create the life you choose to live.

Let's relate Newton's law of motion to our lives. Newton's law states that objects tend to *keep on doing what they're doing* (unless acted upon by an unbalanced force). If at rest, they will *continue in this same state of rest*. All objects *resist changes* in their state of motion!

But *you* are *not* an object... Are you?

You have the ability to change your focus, your goals and your pace. You have the power to control your thoughts and emotions. You are capable to start transforming your life right now (you are not a tree, are you?)

"The bad news is time flies. The good news is you're the pilot."
~Michael Althsuler

"Don't ever let anyone tell you "you can't do something", not even me, alright? You got a dream? You got to protect it. People who can't do it themselves, they wanna tell you "you can't do it". If you want something, Go Get It!" ~Will Smith (The Pursuit of Happyness)

"Everyone needs peace of mind, inner-happiness and joyful relationships but most people don't prioritise these. Do you set goals or invest in learning to achieve these? If you focus only on career, social and financial goals then you will never be fulfilled or fully successful."
~Maddy Malhotra

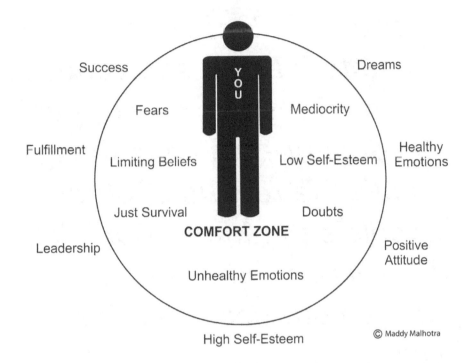

Explore Yourself

If there was one action that you could take immediately to instantly change the quality of your emotions and feelings every day of your life, then what would that be?

Your time is limited, so don't waste it living someone else's life. Don't be trapped by dogma - which is living with the results of other people's thinking. Don't let the noise of other's opinions drown out your own inner voice. And most important, have the courage to follow your heart and intuition. They somehow already know what you truly want to become. Everything else is secondary. ~Steve Jobs

Practical Tips and Techniques to Make Your Life Better

Get started on changing your life for the better right now.

Maybe this is the first time you have really thought about yourself or looked deeply into your life and it may feel weird but if you want to make your life better then you will have to evaluate your assumptions, beliefs, values and priorities. It will be worth the investment.

Today is a good day to start knowing your 'self' and to plan for betterment of your life. When you understand how your beliefs, emotions and thoughts are affecting your attitude, decisions, actions and results, and you change the ones that aren't working for you, then you will see a difference in every area of your life.

Your life is YOUR responsibility

The first step is to become aware of your 'self'. If you have been pondering the Explore Yourself questions in the previous chapters you will already be becoming aware of your 'self', your thoughts and beliefs and your consequential actions.

You'll have started to realise that...

- No miracle may happen.
- No God's angel may come to rescue you.
- You probably won't find Aladdin's magic lamp on a street.
- No one else will take action on your behalf.
- Just wishing or dreaming will not make your life better...

...but taking action will!

A big breakthrough which jolted me out of my trance/illusion /helplessness was realising that nothing will change if I don't take responsibility for my life; if I don't look into my life and if I don't take action to make it better.

Live consciously

Living consciously means being aware and being accountable for where you are in regards to your goals and targets for every area of your life. Self-evaluation and getting feedback from external sources to evaluate the results you are getting, admitting your mistakes and looking for solutions to rectify them. Persevering in adverse situations. Having an open mind to receive new information and willingness to edit or delete old beliefs, rules, habits and assumptions and adding new ones for betterment of your life. Believing that learning is a never ending process. Understanding your needs, purpose, values etc.

Most of us are so lost in the past, watching our same old painful movie again and again, that we forget the solutions exist but they do and we have all the resources we need to find them. Try asking yourself some simple questions to provoke your subconscious into finding those solutions for you.

What can I do to make my condition/situation/life better?

What have I achieved by cursing my past, by hating myself and by blaming people and circumstances?

What can I do to create the life of my dreams in the present and future?

"Will you look back in your life and say 'I wish I had' or 'I'm glad I did'?"
~Zig Ziglar

Become aware of your thought patterns

Your thoughts become your physical reality!

We live in the world of our thoughts all day long. The amount of happiness, success, love, peace and fulfilment you experience and achieve depends on the nature and quality of your thoughts. **The good news is that you can make a conscious choice as to what thoughts you think (what you focus on) and which actions you take (or not take) and to override negative, limiting or disempowering thoughts.**

Take a moment and make a list of people, media and events which influence your day-to-day thoughts.

Many personal development and spiritual gurus suggest that we decrease the time we spend on watching or listening to the daily news because it is full of negative stories; especially if you watch or listen to it every morning then you feed your subconscious mind with a breakfast full of negative stuff and you probably think about some of that throughout the day.

Initially, you may find it difficult to keep track of every thought and they may keep coming back but with practice you will become more aware of them and then can change them for something more helpful and positive if they are unhelpful or disempowering thoughts.

"It is mental discipline to keep certain thoughts out of your head and put certain thoughts in your head. You have conscious control over that. It takes practice and repetition." ~1996 Gold Medal Swimmer

"With self-discipline most anything is possible." ~Theodore Roosevelt

If you need help to identify and control the thoughts that are not serving you and are blocking your path to your success and happiness, then email me for one to one coaching: success@coachmaddy.com

Take control of your self-talk, inner-gremlin or inner-critics

Have you ever questioned your inner-critic? Do you trust it?

What do you say to yourself about:

- Your identity and abilities (appearance, worthiness, competence and intelligence)
- What you deserve in each area of your life
- What would your future be? What are the possibilities in different areas of life?
- What do you say to yourself during difficult situations or while trying something new?

- What does your inner critic say about the life in general? (life is a battle, full of problems, sucks, hell)
- What kind of self-talk do you usually have for others and for the world around you?

In many situations, the only thing you can control is your own response. Changing self-talk from negative to positive is an excellent way to manage that response. We weren't taught that the words we regularly use to describe our experiences and conditions in life impact and influence our emotional states. Use your words wisely and kindly, as you would to your best friend.

Stop blaming yourself. Stop regretting. Stop focusing on the past. Stop listening to people who don't support you and who aren't experiencing happiness, success, peace and fulfilment for themselves. Stop labelling yourself as 'unlucky'. What would your best friend say to you? Ask them! And be your own best friend too.

Our questions determine our thoughts

The questions we ask ourselves, in our head, determine where we focus, how we think, how we feel, and what we decide and/or do. So it's time to ask ourselves better questions.

Try asking questions like these:

Everyone deserves happiness. When am I going to allow myself the happiness I deserve?

How much more am I capable of?

When will I reach my perfect weight, now I am committed to doing what it takes to get there?

How could I find a perfect soul mate? What is really likeable about me?

What could I do right now to make myself feel better and beat this depressed feeling?

Your subconscious starts working to validate what you ask yourself. It looks for evidence and finds references to back it up. So asking questions like 'What can I do to make my condition/situation/ life better?' immediately gets your subconscious working on solutions rather than finding more evidence for the problem.

Evaluate/Challenge your beliefs

YOU need to get better before your life gets better so create a better mindset. Success starts within and stems from your beliefs. Happiness comes from within and depends on your beliefs.

A sad truth is that most of us don't know what we really believe! We don't know what is holding us back. Beliefs have the power to make us successful or not, happy or depressed, loving or criminal. Negative or limiting beliefs limit our ability to achieve the life we desire. Very few of us examine our beliefs critically. So here is an opportunity to do just that.

> *"It's not the events of our lives that shape us, but our beliefs as to what those events mean." ~Tony Robbins*

On a scale of 1-10 check your <u>worth levels</u> by asking: Am I worthy of...

☐ A lot of money/luxury

☐ Being loved

☐ Being promoted / getting more business

☐ Happiness

On a scale of 1-10 check your <u>deserving levels</u> by asking: Do I deserve...

☐ A lot of money/to be rich

☐ An abundance of love

☐ Happiness

☐ A fit body

On a scale of 1-10 check your <u>ability levels</u> by asking: Am I capable of...

☐ Earning lots of money

☐ Attracting the right soul mate

☐ Getting promotion, handling more/larger business

Pick up an area to explore. Write down the challenges/problems you are facing. Then ask yourself, which beliefs of mine are responsible for this? What fears do I have in that area, that are stopping me from achieving desired results?

In detail write down:

What are these beliefs costing me emotionally, physically and/or financially?

What are their negative effects on my relationships and/or profession?

Start writing the beliefs you would like to replace the old ones with. Usually the opposite of the old beliefs works best. Work through each belief and list the benefits that the new beliefs will have. What feelings will the new ones generate?

Be honest and be willing to take the responsibility of your life from this very moment. **Your results will change only when the old false beliefs are replaced with the ones which will serve you for good.** Utilising your power to choose your beliefs consciously and intentionally can improve the quality of every area of your life.

"When you doubt your power, you give power to your doubt."
~Honore de Balzac

"Within you right now is the power to do things you never dreamed possible. This power becomes available to you just as soon as you can change your beliefs." ~Maxwell Maltz

YOUR NOTES

YOUR NOTES

Let's Get Specific

Today, most people want quick and easy results. They don't want to pay the price for achieving success. For years (or their whole lives) they expect miracles to happen or a lottery win perhaps, but 90% of people *never* amount living the life of their dreams... *why?*

Success is a slow and gradual process like a plant which takes months or years to produce fruits. It's the same for every profession whether you're a doctor of medicine, solicitor, painter, singer, entrepreneur, accountant, Olympian... to be honest I have never understood why people even think of quick and easy results... who tells them it's possible, or is it just an excuse to live in their comfort zones?

I have spent thousands of dollars and hours on learning the principles of success and realized two things (for long-term results) –

1. Success in anything takes time, experience, dedication, action and continual learning

2. First we must change our beliefs, habits and attitude and then expect success and fulfilment in life

Becoming Rich

From what I have learnt from my experiences and of other people, there is no quick rich scheme! Please beware of companies or individuals who offer courses, workshops for shares or currency trading, real estate investment, internet marketing etc. because they sell their products by using hypnotic lingo and they make attractive claims like making big money quickly while working part time... Some of them even show you copies of fake testimonials and bank statements! I have met so many people who think just reading a book or attending a course will make them overnight millionaires or help them become rich by working just 4 hours a week!

You will have to be an ever ready learner. If you have a day job you will have to learn technical skills as well as communication, management, leadership skills etc. to climb the ladder of success. If you are a business owner you need to do a lot more than just being good at what you do, i.e. marketing and sales skills will be the most required and of course some risk will be involved.

However, all this shouldn't stop you from achieving your dreams.

"If you want to be rich... don't allow yourself the luxury of excuses."
~Robert Kiyosaki

When I asked Keith Cunningham (a billionaire), during a seminar in London, about using money properly he said "never ever use other people's money to buy luxury for yourself." What he meant was, don't take loans or use over draft or credit card money to buy pleasure. He also mentioned that he uses other people's money to invest in order to build wealth.

"Too many people spend money they haven't earned, to buy things they don't want, to impress people they don't like." ~Will Smith (actor)

Fill in the blanks:

Rich people are ____

The maximum I can earn per year is ____

I can become rich / make more money only if ____

If I have a lot of money people will think I am ____

(If any of the answers, you have written above, are limiting or negative then your chances of becoming rich are minimal.)

Am I in control of my life? Do I take responsibility of my life? If not, then why?

Do I stop myself doing things because I have a fear of rejection? If yes, then why?

Will I ever be able to become rich? If not, then why?

Do I stop myself doing things because I have a fear of rejection? If yes, then why?

For your finances/career or business growth, write down the beliefs which aren't serving you. Then for each problem and related beliefs ask yourself - Which beliefs would serve me better? Then write the beliefs you would like to replace the old ones with.

*practical exercises in this book have been taken from Maddy's *home study course.*

YOUR NOTES

YOUR NOTES

Gaining Confidence

Psychologists rarely use the word 'self-confidence' they use terms like self-efficacy, self-esteem, self-reliance, self-worth etc. Self-confidence is how you feel about your abilities i.e. the beliefs you hold about your capability to perform tasks in various areas of life.

You will have to deal with your fears in order to increase confidence and progress in life. Stop predicting your future and stop procrastinating while in your comfort zone because of the limiting beliefs and doubts you hold. Don't let average/mediocre people tell you what you cannot do!

Beware, some people you may come across (wear a mask) as bold and confident. That doesn't mean their self-esteem is high or they are happy within. A lot of over-achievers have low self-love too!

*"There is only one security, and when you've lost that security, you've lost everything you've got. And that is the security of **confidence** in yourself; to be, to create, to make any position you want to make for yourself. And when you lose that confidence, you've lost the only security you can have. Self-confidence is self-determinism. One's belief in one's ability to determine his own course. As long as one has that, he's got the universe in his pocket. And when he hasn't got that, not all the pearls in China nor all the grain and corn in Iowa can give him security, because that's the only security there is." ~L. Ron Hubbard*

Remember:

✓ No one is born with confidence
✓ Even if you had a rough childhood you can still have high confidence level
✓ Don't let other people's negative criticisms from the past impact your self-confidence today

- ✓ Many people are nervous in social situations but that doesn't mean you aren't confident in other situations. You can overcome social anxiety at will
- ✓ You don't have to be smart, thin, attractive (fill in the blank) to be self-confident
- ✓ Be kind to your inner self

Explore Yourself

What do you repeat in your mind about your confidence levels? and whether you will be able to increase confidence in the future?

Ideal Body

What I have learnt from my experiences and of other people, there is no weight-loss technique which is healthy and works overnight!

Are you aware of the facts for diet and exercise? Which is truly good for your body and which one is an over-marketed product/technique? Is it fat, calories or carbohydrates which need cutting down? Is it yoga, aerobics or jogging which will burn the harmful fat and not damage your body in the long-term? Is it a crash diet, water diet or low carb diet which will naturally reduce weight without too much stress and pressure on the body?

Remember: gyms, dieticians, cosmetic surgery companies, pharmaceutical companies… they are all businesses and they will usually think of their profit before your health.

Please think of the long-term consequences, and remind yourself that natural processes are slow, before considering surgeries which may offer quick weight loss tricks, or dieticians that ask you to perform abnormal activities or the PE/Gym trainers who suggest extreme workouts!

As I mentioned in the goal setting chapter, you must work on your self-beliefs, habits, and related repetitive thoughts first (root cause). Usually, people are over weight due to emotional issues and/or negative self-beliefs which are created because of painful past events or mistakes or failures. Once you have looked in to it then set your goals. Be confident, and frequently remind yourself of the benefits of achieving your goals.

If you don't work on your mindset, chances are you will gain it back and/or you still won't like yourself after losing weight!

Whether its binge eating (emotional eating) or anorexia or bulimia or an obsession for gym (I categorise all these practices as 'Self-harm').

A widely accepted theory is that people develop these disorders because they seek control over themselves and their lives. A high percentage of people struggling with these disorders have a history of abuse, neglect, or other traumatic experiences, and develop these as coping mechanisms.

"There are 3 billion woman who don't look like supermodels and only 8 who do." ~The Body Shop

Dieting has become an unfortunate cultural trend, especially for girls and women. Their self image is often closely linked with their body image. Unfortunately, the message that thinner is better is affecting younger children too. They think <u>thinness</u> brings confidence and attention.

What sought of bad culture (neurotic society) are we developing?

Self-esteem has nothing to do with your body shape, period. The solution to the problems in your current life or painful past events has nothing to do with your food or physical appearance, it's a vicious circle!

Genuine respect and gratitude for your body is essential in order to heal yourself and feel happy for your body. Think how blessed you are as compared to the humans who are disabled or have major diseases. Please don't take your body for granted. We live in a society where we experience a lot of stress and negative emotions and on top of it if you punish your body with too much exercise or starvation, then what would happen to your body?

Don't let self-blame, negative criticisms from others or guilt hold you back. Focus on achieving your ideal weight/shape. Make sure you lose weight for yourself not for others or for an occasion. Don't become obsessed by media and social judgement, i.e. some women keep doing, unnecessary, heavy workouts even after achieving their ideal weight/shape. Please start respecting your body.

For women

I request you not to go crazy for exercising and/or dieting. If you exercise and change your food/eating habits, please do it a natural way. Changes in nature are slow. Fat piles up slowly, so burn it slowly. I hear about and coach so many women who go beyond the normal to change their appearance. Rather than respecting their bodies, they harm themselves with too much exercise and/or eating too little.

If you want a healthy, nice body, then let it take its time. Don't starve and don't go for crazy carb-burning exercises, please! Rather, work on accepting yourself, changing your definition/beliefs about 'looking good' and please do not copy the celebrities. Perfectionism and/or approval addiction will kill you!

> *"I feel it is important not to get overly obsessed and overly carried away with just the physical aspect. There is more to beauty than just the physical appearance. You are also a complete person, and a woman should have an identity beyond just the way she looks."* ~Katrina Kaif Turcotte
> (Celebrated Actress, Listed 4 times in the FHM 100 Sexiest Women in the World, Inspiring Role Model, Wax figure at Madame Tussauds London, Philanthropist)

Genuinely happy and healthy people never look for instant gratification. They know that quick results will not last long and will not be healthy, no matter what area of life it is.

If you keep punishing your body by over-exercising and/or under-eating, what do you expect in return from your body?

The statistics for exercise addiction, under-eating and self-hate are alarming, and what's more shocking is the number of teenagers who are anxious and worried about their appearance and confidence levels.

Is it the media that is making us feel/look inferior by repeatedly showing the celebrities who try to seek attention by looking different than the crowd? Or is it the adverts of cosmetic companies, gyms and beauty salons, which indirectly tell us that we aren't good enough?

You do need fat, calories, carbohydrates and sugar for surviving. Just choose the right ones in right amounts as prescribed by qualified health practitioners/nutritionists.

A lot of men (and some women) build muscles because of low self-esteem. When the need of attention is at peak, people opt for gyms, get tattoos, get pierced, run very long distance marathons, and indulge in dangerous adventures and other activities which may not be good for their bodies.

Please be good to your body. Value it. Too much exercise, extra protein supplements etc. can't be good in long-term. I remember when I used to work night shifts as an IT consultant, there were many men who used to go to the office gym at 1, 2 or 3am and then have proper meal or supplements, early in the morning, after their workout!

Do you think that can be good for a body? It's too far away from natural living!

Will I ever be able to – gain my ideal weight/body shape/heal my body? If not, then why?

Do I love and accept myself? If not, then why?

For your Fitness, write down the beliefs which aren't serving you. Then for each problem and related beliefs ask yourself – What beliefs would serve me better? Writing the beliefs you would like to replace the old ones with.

*practical exercises in this book have been taken from Maddy's *home study course*.

YOUR NOTES

Happy Relationships

In the beginning, most couples experience great fun, excitement and intimacy. Each lover is on their best behavior, showing affection and kindness. For a few months/weeks, the expectations and needs are met easily and often.

However, things start changing, and it feels that extra effort is required to keep the spark. Gradually, they feel that the spark is gone. Along the way, they create lots of beliefs, usually negative, about their partners and find out that the relationship is not a solution to their problems, which at the beginning of commitment, they thought it was!

Some, at this point, move on to another person, some start looking for fulfilment from other potential partners and some continue to drag out their fruitless relationship.

It's because they don't understand the root cause of the issues and no one taught them how relationships work! Also, a lot of unhappy people don't want to make an extra effort to rejuvenate their relationships because they expect easy work around and, more precisely, they want their partner to change/improve as per their expectations (like most of us, they expect things to happen quickly and easily in every area of our lives).

"Each relationship nurtures a strength or weakness within you."
~Mike Murdock

Relationships evolve and dissolve for mutual benefits. Challenges in relationships (and in every area of life) are inevitable, no matter what the 'law of attraction' and 'positive' gurus say! People dream of a perfect life and feel disappointed and frustrated because difficulties keep showing up. I think younger people usually have an unrealistic expectation of what lies ahead at the time of committing to a relationship.

"Some of the biggest challenges in relationships come from the fact that most people enter a relationship in order to get something: they're trying to find someone who's going to make them feel good. In reality, the only way a relationship will last is if you see your relationship as a place that you go to give, and not a place that you go to take." ~Anthony Robbins

What do you think is the biggest barrier that keeps people from having the relationship they want?

Is it beliefs (rules for how to live life and how relationships should be or how men/women must behave in a relationship), expectations, stubbornness, lack of input, lack of commitment to improve/resolve, perfectionism, fears or bad habits?

You may be aware of many reasons. Let's discuss the core ones:

Values and Beliefs – We aren't aware of the fact that we all have our own unique set of beliefs, values, experiences, habits and perceptions, which means how one of the partners thinks about the world can be completely different than the other. It also means that the definition of happiness, success, love, socializing, right and wrong may differ for both of them, so don't expect them to work in harmony automatically. If we understand this concept, which I am sure you do now after reading the previous chapters, and keep this in mind each time we have a conflict or difficulty in making decisions, we would be more compassionate and respectful for each other. How great would that be?

Attention and Genuine Praise – These are our basic emotional needs. We are all hungry for appreciation and attention, but unfortunately, most of us experience a lack of attention and praise during our childhoods! Some partners think that rather than giving regular time, attention and appreciation, they can get away with buying occasional gifts in order to keep their partner happy, but does that work? Can material objects, nice dinners or clothes increase inner fulfillment and love? No. It can only give temporary gratification/pleasure and may just drag a relationship.

The way partners give (and receive) attention and praise affects intimacy, fulfilment and respect in relationships, so be genuine and express yourself in a nice and loving tone. Make appreciation a habit. A lot of people say, "I love you," or "You look nice," just for the sake of it. They need to know that love resides in your heart, not in your left brain, so let it flow from its origin.

Some of us weren't hugged/cuddled enough. A lack of loving touch can be bad for emotional health, too. So, hug and be creative; maybe try it with various expressions and caring words.

Compassion and Empathy – I read somewhere that "compassion is a virtue that follows from empathy." Judging each other based on your beliefs is not going to be positive. One must be aware of the beliefs, experiences and values of the other to really understand why his/her partner is reacting, behaving or deciding in a certain way. Their reasons may sound illogical, but that doesn't mean they are wrong or less intelligent. It just means they may need to alter their beliefs and re-align their values. So, before you feel 'put off' by your partner's response to difficulties, try to be in their shoes and analyse why they feel in a certain way. If you can empathise and avoid judgment, it will allow you to feel compassionate and offer support in a loving and kind way.

When you are more compassionate, your communication with each other will improve, too.

Professor Simon Cohen, in his research, concluded that "women are more likely to empathise and men usually like to systemise, but there is every potential for that to be reversed in an individual."

When an argument starts changing into a personal attack, one must stop and analyse the root cause of the reactions/behavior and wait for a few minutes or hours before discussing the topic again. You don't have to resolve issues or criticise while you are in a negative state of mind.

It is vital that you resolve conflicts constructively.

139

Control your reaction by conditioning your mind every single day. Tell your mind that you have never gained happiness, peace or love by arguing or reacting badly, and also remember the fact that negative emotions harm your body!

Make a 'love journal' and write down what needs changing in whom and review it every week.

Social Programming – Comparison is one of the biggest negative habits we are taught and unconsciously learn as kids, and this habit continues to influence every area of our lives. Our attitude, emotions and decisions are all affected by *comparing* people, things and ourselves.

"Studies done on the **contrast principle** suggest that we may be less satisfied with the physical attractiveness of our own lovers because of the way the popular media bombard us with examples of unrealistically attractive models," says Dr. Robert Cialdini.

I agree with the above statement, and it isn't just physical attractiveness. We compare qualities, lifestyles, material possessions and social behaviour of our partners with other couples but never explore whether or not those celebrities or other couples really experience inner joy, true love and peace!

"The truth is, unless you let go, unless you forgive yourself, unless you forgive the situation, unless you realize that the situation is over, you cannot move forward." ~Steve Maraboli

Accept *what is* before you start working on yourself and each other. Remember this: you cannot change your partner unless he/she wants to change, and if they chose to, then they will improve in their own time. All you can do is motivate and encourage them, be patient and supportive.

Accept the fact that ups are as much part of life as the downs. Learn to ride the waves together if you wish to become a genuinely happy couple. Ask questions to analyse the issues rather than telling your partner what is right. Men, you don't know everything; accept it. Women, stop being a professional worrier and stop holding onto fears. (Clearly, I am generalising here!)

To create and keep a happy relationship, the partners must ensure that there is space for each of them to learn, change and grow. Stagnancy is like death! Both the partners must invest time, energy and money in personal development and for the betterment of their relationship. Commitment involves loyalty, mutual trust and maintaining an interest in each other's goals.

"Life is not about waiting for the storms to pass. It's about learning how to dance in the rain." ~Vivian Greene

Like exercise is necessary to keep your body fit, similarly, regular reinvigorating is required to keep relationships joyful and fun. Don't play the 'you do it first, and then I will' game. Lovingly give what you most wish to receive.

There are many books and seminars that can help you to create a fulfilling and juicy relationship, or you can <u>contact me</u> for coaching where we can do everything listed in this chapter, set effective goals and monitor your progress. Email: love@coachmaddy.com

"If people refuse to look at you in a new light and they can only see you for what you were, only see for the mistakes you've made, if they don't realize that you are not your mistakes, then they have to go." ~Steve Maraboli

"Some people believe holding on and hanging in there are signs of great strength. However, there are times when it takes much more strength to know when to let go and then do it." ~Ann Landers

Genuinely thank each other often. Show gratitude for everything you can because a lot is taken for granted!

Make a list of different ways for:

How can you create memories together?

How can you add more juice/spark to your relationship?

How you can give your partner some loving attention? (e.g. - send cards, romantic texts, express what you like about them etc.)

Have you forgotten the good times, the gifts and exchange of love which occurred in the past? Do you thank for it now? Do you cherish the memories?

How much happier could you be if there was more laughter in your relationship? What can you do, learn or say regularly which can increase humor in your relationship?

Write you beliefs/rules about: how a relationship should be, romance, trust and happiness in a relationship. Then figure out what needs tweaking or deleting.

Do you expect perfectionism from your partner?

Are there any beliefs, which you created in your childhood about men/women/partners/relationships, which stop you from experiencing intimacy, happiness, love or fun in your relationship?

How does pushing each other's emotional triggers increase love, joy and juice in your relationship? Whenever you argue or push your partner's emotional buttons, ask yourself: am I doing it to prove my self/ego right? Is it about who wins the argument? Are these habits good for me and my partner's health?

Practice 'love making' rather than just physical pleasure.

Write at least 10 ways to deal with boredom. Keep in mind, variety is a basic human need.

We all like to be rewarded so reward each other for improving, even if it's a little step towards betterment. Write at least 5 different ways of rewarding (it doesn't have to be an expensive gift).

Perform a quarterly/half-yearly assessment. If possible, go to a nice peaceful place for a few days and, like mature/sensible adults: check your progress, changes in circumstances and mindset, and issues which have come up and need resolving.

Visualisation can do wonders. It can motivate you and make you feel positive. Believe in each other's goals and together, visualise positive possibilities.

YOUR NOTES

YOUR NOTES

YOUR NOTES

Trying to be happy by accumulating possessions is like trying to satisfy hunger by taping sandwiches all over your body.
~George Carlin
(5 times Grammy award winner)

Experience Real Happiness

Most of us don't understand what happiness really is and keep seeking it from wrong sources

Have you ever thought about what makes you happy? I mean after you have taken care of the basic needs like house, bills, food, clothes, etc.?

Is your happiness dependant on the outside world (i.e. people, possessions etc.)?

Do you use distractions, like watching TV, surfing the Internet, going on holidays and/or consume alcohol, smoke or self-harm to mask your misery/unhappiness?

Yes? It means you are looking for happiness outside of yourself!

It's similar to self-esteem, which most people try to build from external sources. You are stuck in a never-ending loop, you are addicted because the more you get, the more you need to maintain your happiness. The positive feelings from outside are temporary!

Because of this dependence of ours, the advertisements these days are designed accordingly. They want us to buy their products to feel or look good. We are all being programmed by repeated adverts, songs and TV programs to look for positive emotions and esteem outside ourselves.

Which beliefs make you buy the things you do?

Do you know an 'emotional shopper?' A client of mine used to go out and shop each time she felt miserable or depressed, even when she had no money of her own and later would cry and panic when the credit card and overdraft bills arrived. Can you guess what she did to avoid the pain (apart from blaming herself in her head)? She would engage in more shopping, drink alcohol and sometimes physically harm herself, too!

Do you use the bank's money to buy pleasure or luxury?

Yes? You are highly likely to experience negative emotions and self-blame.

If happiness could be bought, all the people we see on the TV and read about in the newspapers and magazines would be the happiest people... but are they?

No, most of them are not! (The same goes for inner-peace and love.)

No sports/posh car, big mansion or luxurious sofa comes with a guarantee of making you feel blissful/joyful! It may give you some kind of temporary satisfaction, happiness and/or peace of mind.

People spend money to feel good or distract themselves from unwanted thoughts and emotions. There is nothing wrong with having lots of possessions or escaping to relax, *but* these aren't a solution to any personal issues.

We are free to choose happiness. We have the ability to be happy or unhappy. These days, happiness is unbelievable and unusual. For example when I was employed and walked in to the office in the morning, my colleagues would ask, "How are you doing Maddy?"

I replied with, "I am happy," or "I am joyful" or anything similar. They use to look at me like I was from a different planet or would say, "Are you on drugs?"

Human beings are aware of two options: happiness and misery but trees and birds aren't aware of the latter which is why they stay happy most of the time. Have you ever heard a bird saying, "I am in a bad mood, so I will scream or cry today?" Or have the flowers ever said, "I am angry, so I will stink today?"

Usually, we aren't happy because we lack harmony in our lives and we don't enjoy what we do. Loving our work and the way of living is also a type of meditation.

We choose our ways, but they are rarely happy because we don't follow what our heart desires. We are much occupied with acquiring money, status and power. There are many small things that can make us happy like the song of a bird, a beautiful butterfly, colourful and smiling flowers or a cool breeze. These things can't give us money or social status, but they can become sources of happiness. Happy and satisfied people choose their way and don't complain about it. One can think, "I am rich because I am happy."

"If you aren't happy for what you already have then what makes you think you will be happy with more" ~Maddy Malhotra

People lose their true self when they run after money, fame or power. They forget the intrinsic values of life i.e. bliss, peace, love... they satisfy their ego and social needs on the expense of discarding their core nature.

A positive attitude and determination to be happy is required to be truly successful, but most people do the opposite by talk/thinking about misery all the time. Some are happy to pay for a psychotherapist or counsellor, buy antidepressants or medication for pains/diseases and spend for instant gratification/avoidance rather than changing their mindsets!

Misery in an area of life doesn't make you a bad person. In fact, the underlying beliefs (fears and habits) that you learned weren't good and healthy for you. Create your own beliefs and decide to be happy because rules and instructions from other people may not benefit you.

Are Pleasure, Happiness and Bliss/Joy the Same?

What is Pleasure?

Many of us think, "Pleasure and happiness are the same." The next section covers happiness in detail, but in short, 'pleasure' is experienced through our senses whereas happiness is psychological. People try to achieve everything through their body, which is actually not possible.

Pain and pleasure go hand in hand. If you experience pleasure, you will feel pain, too. This is how the universe works. When most people experience pleasure, they have a fear of losing it, too, and when they are in pain, they make every possible effort to come out of that. This vicious cycle continues forever. They run from one sensory pleasure to another. They live at the basic level.

We live in a world of duality (i.e. day/night, life/death, good/evil, rich/poor, positive/negative, etc.). Each pleasure is balanced by the same amount of pain. Most of us are unaware about this fact, but most of us aren't ready to face pain while we keep running after momentary pleasures.

Seeker of pleasure remain at the mercy of the outside world because pleasure is always related to something else (e.g. people, things, circumstances, etc.), which makes them a slave who live in a prison by choice!

"I hope everybody could get rich and famous, and have everything they
ever dreamed of, so they will know that it's not the answer."
~Jim Carrey (actor)

Few people find pleasure in money. The more they get, the more they become dependent on it because they have a fear of losing it, and the cycle continues. When we seek pleasure in the food we eat, we get bored by the specific tastes because gradually, our taste buds will not respond to the taste, and we will feel bad or look for variety. It's the same for relationships based on pleasures. One can have a good time with someone, but that doesn't last for long because the amount of pleasure will decrease and the pains will show up, too. Unfortunately a lot of people, especially the young ones, think that sex is a key to happiness. They are stuck in a nasty loop because the desire is never ending and unfulfilling. The real need is of love making but people aren't aware of the difference between sex and making love!

We have a desire to have a nice, big house, and once we have it, our minds will start seeking something else after the initial euphoria fades because there is no limit to pleasure-seeking. People become victims of unlimited desires, which lead to restlessness and fearfulness.

What is Happiness?

Happiness is more human and cultured than pleasure; it comes from quality, not quantity. It's psychological, not physiological and not a relief from some kind of suffering because it's a sort of enrichment. This state can be attained by listening to music, watching kids or animals, making love or looking/connecting with the beauty of the nature. This is something much deeper and higher than the pleasure you gain from sex, food, money or material. However, it's temporary.

Mike was 32, married and worked as an office administrator in London. He wanted more money, hope and, of course, happiness. He tried to work extra hours, played the lottery and considered online business as well but couldn't buy much for him and his partner. He suffered with low moods, anxiety and occasional depression. However, things changed when his grandfather died and left him $700,000.

He paid off his mortgage and credit cards, bought a nice car and bought a luxurious holiday package. He was happy, and so was his partner. His confidence increased, and negative emotions decreased quite a lot.

As the months passed, his happiness and self-esteem started dropping, and within eighteen months, his emotional health was same as before. Why did that happen even though his financial worries were next to none, and he was living a better life overall?

Like career or business success, like body weight, like financial success and like self-love, we have a thermostat/range for our happiness and misery levels, too. It depends on our personal beliefs/rules, which define happiness and how happy we can be. These beliefs can make people experience negative emotions, even when they have it all and can make some people feel happy and motivated, even if they had a road accident or loss in their recent past.

"The world has to learn that the actual pleasure derived from material things is of rather low quality on the whole and less even in quantity than it looks to those who have not tried it." ~Oliver Wendell Holmes

In his bestselling book, Dr. Martin Seligman has listed many researches for temporary and long-term happiness. In a nutshell, studies show factors, such as wealth, physical attractiveness, high-paying jobs, physical health and negative events have a low impact on our happiness levels!

Isn't that surprising? Are you thinking that most of us are trying hard to achieve happiness the wrong way?

YES! We have been programmed by big businesses and the media to seek happiness outside of us and in tangible things.

"The more rules you have about how people have to be, how life has to be for you to be happy, the less happy you're going to be!"
~Anthony Robbins

Are you waiting for your life to be perfect before you allow yourself to be happy?

What is Bliss/Joy?

Bliss is neither physiological nor psychological. It's your innermost being where no ego exists. You can reach there just by dissolving your ego and following your truth. You cannot create or invent it. It's the innermost part of you, but our conditioning (beliefs) takes us away from our real self. Bliss makes you a master of your self and free. Self-realisation, becoming one with the existence and achieving the state of Buddha or Zen are some commonly used terms. To experience bliss, you need to be more conscious about yourself. A conscious person cannot be angry, possessive, greedy and ambitious. Consciousness releases the energy involved in all the above activities, and one becomes a magnetic field, which attracts all positive things in life. When you go beyond expectations, you start experiencing bliss and true happiness. Bliss is unconditional.

I do understand that it's difficult to implement this in today's world, but this is how people have been experiencing bliss for thousands of years!

It is very important to distinguish your momentary happiness from long-term happiness. There are many ways to induce momentary happiness (chocolate, comedy films, flowers, playing with pets or children, new clothes, etc).

The challenge is to discover the source of long-term happiness (bliss) and to access it.

The logical minds may think, "Increase the amount of short-term happiness," but it won't be good enough because the sources for both types are different.

If you want to reduce your dependence on external things to make you happy, design your life to generate your joy from within. The great thing about internal joy is that it doesn't cost you any money, and no one can ever take it away from you except you.

"Happiness is the result of circumstances, but Joy endures in spite of circumstances." ~ancient proverb

How to be Happy Today

1. Focus on here and now

If you are not happy today, chances are you will never be! The past is gone and the future is just an imagination. The reality is now.
You have three choices in any given moment:
a) <u>Dwell on the past</u> – Most people do this often. The unanswered questions, the pains, the failures, the injustice, the insults, the abuse, the bereavements... There is no end to this tape, and it keeps playing day and night repeatedly. The past exists no more. You invite unhappiness.

b) <u>Dream about the future</u> – Usually, the thoughts about the future are full of doubts, worries, fears, uncertainty and misery. However, there are people who set positive goals and work on them, but research shows that most of them have more negative/painful/unhealthy thoughts about their future than positive possibilities/accomplishments because our beliefs mould our thoughts. You invite misery and may attract it, too!

c) <u>Live in the now.</u> – Be thankful for all that you have. Believe me, you have at least <u>500</u> things to be thankful for, even if you live an average life in a western country.

People pursuing happiness cannot get it because it happens suddenly and out of nowhere. When I was writing this chapter, I saw a beautiful seagull outside my window, and was lost in its activities. That moment was full of happiness for me. Happiness is always available to you, but when you see it, you miss it. The desire for happiness moves you away from here and now because you move somewhere in the future, which is a dream for you. It shows you aren't happy at the moment and are a miserable being.

"If you are depressed you are living in the past. If you are anxious you are living in the future. If you are at peace you are living in the present."
~Lao Tzu

Enjoy the present. Joseph Veroff and Fred Bryant call it 'savouring' (i.e. the awareness of pleasure and the conscious/purposeful attention to the experience of pleasure). For example, people spoil the joy of a beautiful sunset by taking pictures, talking with others or recalling something from their past. The moment(s) has to be experienced in detail to feel inner joy. You can just be at a beach and see things how they are, or you can feel the cold air you breath in, notice the aroma, the colours, listen to the laughter of others and the sounds of waves, get lost in the vastness, gaze at the lavender sky or the shapes of clouds, feel the peace, the warmth of the sun, the texture of sand, watch the kids play in joy and appreciate/be thankful for what is.

This is what ancient wisdom, especially Buddhism, teach us: *awareness*. Appreciating and enjoying the 'now' has been suggested in Hinduism, Sufism, Buddhism and other beliefs based on meditation and self-realization.

"Happiness cannot be travelled to, owned, earned, worn or consumed. Happiness is the spiritual experience of living every minute with love, grace and gratitude." ~Denis Waitley

After four years of study, a monk arrives at the dwelling of his teacher. He enters the room, bursting with ideas about knotty issues of Buddhist metaphysics and well-prepared for the deep questions that await him in his examination. "I have one question," his teacher intones.

"I am ready, master," he replies.

"In the doorway, were the flowers to the left or to the right of the umbrella?" The monk retires, abashed, for four more years of study.

2. Be yourself:

People don't like happy people because it hurts their egos. They are surprised because they are unable to understand how that person came out of misery. If everyone is in misery, how can one person be so strong and determined? Usually, people don't dare to go against misery. Unhappy people are part of a crowd, but if somebody is happy, he is individual. The greatest happiness in this world is being yourself. A human child is the most helpless child in the whole animal kingdom because he cannot survive without the support of parents and other relations. Naturally powerful people will mould him according to their own mindsets. Most of the people have personalities that are against their desires, and they are pretending to be what they aren't. They were never allowed to be themselves and were forced to live according to someone else's rules and nature. They know that they have been forced to become doctor, engineer, scientist, etc. Few beggars use children as commodities as the source of income. Everyone has been used as a commodity, more or less, because it's happening with everyone at different scales.

People aren't happy because they are being taught everything but how to be themselves. This is a big cause of misery. They have to do a job they don't want to, they have to wear certain type of clothes at work or social gatherings or they may have to marry someone whom they don't truly love. Society has programmed us to be miserable, and it doesn't allow us to express our misery. We are not allowed to be ourselves; hence, there is no peace within!

Sooner or later, you have to come out of this unwanted loop and say, "I want to be myself and not pretend to be someone else." This is a declaration of your freedom. You don't have to be a sheep/part of the crowd that negates inner peace, happiness and the lives of others. You don't need any mask to simply be yourself. That's the beginning of true happiness.

3. Drop your ego:

If you want to genuinely do something, like painting, dancing, engineering or anything else, drop your ego completely. The existence flows through your work, and that's not a race because it's just a creation through you. An artist painting for fame has to defeat all other painters who also want to do the same. This approach brings your work to the secondary position because it's not your priority interest. Ultimately, his work will be ordinary because he cannot do anything extraordinary through competition.

Do things because it makes you feel good or gives you fulfillment, not because of competition, to show off your abilities, to prove yourself superior or to gain fame. I know we are taught to compete since childhood. We are compared to others and office politics makes us competitive, but that's not how positive happiness is generated! Being happy at the expense of someone else's happiness is inhuman. Finding faults in others doesn't prove them wrong and make you right. Help others to be happy. That will actually increase your happiness, and remember, like attracts like.

"The basic thing is that everyone wants happiness, no one wants suffering. And happiness mainly comes from our own attitude, rather than from external factors. If your own mental attitude is correct, even if you remain in a hostile atmosphere, you feel happy." ~Dalai Lama

A win-win deal to create internal happiness is to help others unconditionally. I always suggest my clients to take some time out to contribute to society, not just give money to charities, because of the positive effects of helping others on their emotional health and performance, which also affects their relationships and self-esteem and makes them appreciate who they have. Read more in the contribution chapter. To see me in action and the list of charities, NPOs and projects I support, go to the 'about me' page of www.CaochMaddy.com

Explore Yourself

Make a list of all the external things or other beings that you depend on to avoid pain/misery or to make you happy.

Do you try to buy happiness?

Analyse, why you buy what you buy. Observe the advertisements that promise to increase your happiness, directly or indirectly. Think deeply if those products really increase happiness in the long run

What beliefs/rules do you have about happiness?

How can you be happy?

How can a relationship be joyful?

Are you are waiting for things in the future to make you happy? Do you tell yourself:

I will be happy when I _____

I will be happy when he/she/they _____

I will be happy if _____

Ask yourself:

Do I know for sure that rich people are happy/blissful within?

Do I know for a fact that rich people experience inner-peace?

Am I 100% certain that Olympic medalists, beautiful models, media personalities, best singers and actors, millionaires.. are all fulfilled/thankful/love-full?

YOUR NOTES

3 Keys to Fulfilment, Peace and Healing

This chapter is about increasing fulfilment, inner peace, and love in life. Unfortunately, emotion management and happiness skills are not taught at school or home. What makes me sad is that people today (especially the youth) think that those temporary feelings whilst they are under the influence of alcohol or drugs, is 'joy' and believe that substance abuse is the quickest way to deal with negative emotions or confidence/esteem issues in life.

"Others can't give you inner-peace. Your children, spouse, priest or friends can't give it to you. You have to create it yourself."
~Maddy Malhotra

"A lot of people say they want to get out of pain, and I'm sure that's true, but they aren't willing to make healing a high priority. They aren't willing to look inside to see the source of their pain in order to deal with it."
~Lindsay Wagner

"Healing takes courage, and we all have courage, even if we have to dig a little to find it." ~Tori Amos

Key no. 1 - **Forgiveness**

A wise man once sat in the audience and cracked a joke all of them laughed like crazy. After a moment he cracked the same joke again and a little less people laughed this time. He cracked the same joke third time and no one laughed. He smiled and said "when you can't laugh on the same joke again and again then why do you keep crying over the same things over and over again".

A lot of people say "How can I forgive him/her, they gave me so much pain, they abused me, they didn't help me in need, they killed my pet, they murdered... I wish something bad would happen to her/him, I will make her/him pay, I try my best to avoid her/him...

By not forgiving or letting go whom are you punishing? Who is still feeling bad weeks, months, years after the incident, event? *you*!

Don't blame yourself for not knowing about your beliefs. Whatever you did in the past was a result of unawareness of the facts you are learning here. Get excited about what you are going to create. Re-inventing yourself can be fun.

"Forgiveness isn't something we do for other people. We do it for ourselves, to get well and move on." ~unknown

There are quotes and I have heard many people saying 'forget' the incidents and move on. Trying to forget is just another means of denial and whatever is denied is not forgiven. I don't think that works in the long-term. Suppressing those thoughts and attached emotions will bounce back. Deal with it and let go. You don't delete those memories you just minimise the emotional affects.

"Anyone can hold a grudge, but it takes a person with character to forgive. When you forgive, you release yourself from a painful burden. Forgiveness doesn't mean what happened was OK, and it doesn't mean that person should still be welcome in your life. It just means you have made peace with the pain, and are ready to let it go." ~Unknown

164

Remember, you are not doing a favour to someone who gave you pain, but that you are being merciful to yourself. To carry anger against anyone is to poison your own heart, releasing toxins each time you replay those memories in your mind.

When you ask yourself whether someone deserves your forgiveness, you are asking the wrong question. Ask instead whether you deserve to become someone who forgives because it's your happiness and peace which is affected by re-playing those incidents/experiences in your mind.

"To forgive is to set a prisoner free and discover that the prisoner was you." ~Lewis Smedes

I can tell you by experience that it feels incredible when you forgive and let go. Yes those emotions, pictures, sounds and places will come in front of you but for the good. My self-esteem healed when I forgave myself for so many things which weren't even logical!

Be compassionate with yourself and forgive yourself each time that guilt, regret or self-blame comes in to mind. There is no logic in driving a car using the back mirror!

Affirmations you may repeat in your mind or out loud -
I love myself
I let go of _____
(If you are religious) The forgiveness of God is always available to me.

"When you forgive people, event, circumstances, you are in the process of change which leads you towards your final destination which is Love. Toxic energies are replaced with healthy positive energies." ~Dr Hew Len

"Healing doesn't mean the damage never existed. It means the damage no longer controls our lives." ~unknown

Letting go of the old ties

Emotions are strange things, we don't just feel them in the moment they get stuck in the body attached to our memories. In order to fully let them go we also need to revisit some of those memories and 'amend' them so they no longer have the emotions attached to them – they are merely the event. This exercise will help that process.

With whom are you holding onto past grievances / resentments that trigger unhealthy emotions in you?

Who do you need to forgive?

Who or what do you need to let go of?

What have these ties cost up till date?

What would they cost you if you don't cut them?

How and which areas of your life will improve if you let these ties go?

Are you absolutely committed to making this change in your life/mind?

Make forgiveness a daily ritual. If you can't prioritise it daily then, at least, do it weekly. Make 'letting-go' a habit.

Key no. 2 - **Gratitude**

"We tend to forget that happiness doesn't come as a result of getting something we don't have, but rather of recognizing and appreciating what we do have." ~Frederick Keonig

The best attitude you can possibly seek is one of appreciation and gratitude. Do you think it's fair to keep asking for more and complaining and not being thankful for what you have?

Challenges make us strong and are an opportunity for learning and growth. Try to thank for the challenges as they serve as building blocks in our lives. I know it's hard but believe me it will make you life happier and positive. And each time you want to feel good, feel blessed or feel lucky then change your focus while facing challenge(s) i.e. think of all you have in life. Count every tiny thing, caring friends and family, body parts, think of those in the third world who don't have the wealth, education, health and basic necessities **you are privileged to have**.

"Wake up with a heart that is grateful because having a grateful heart is the secret to a life of happiness. Life is too short for one to dwell on all that's wrong." ~Brigitte Nicole

These days many life coaches and motivational speakers tell us to 'thank more to have more' and people start thanking for things they have but do they get more of it? NO! The same teachers also tell you to 'visualise and ask the universe for the things you want and they will show up (manifest) in your life', millions of people have tried with no luck! Why?

You must *feel* and *believe* only then you will manifest things or connect with the right people. Without positive and strong beliefs attached with positive emotions you will not be able to achieve much success or fulfillment in life.

We all desire for more... I wish I had, If I could, If only I... and forget about what we already have. Most people blame, complain or curse their luck and wish they could find Aladdin's lamp or a magic wand, they pity themselves, they love to talk about their problems... because they never think about or see all the good things they have.

"Remind yourself daily that someone somewhere is happy with less than you possess." ~Maddy Malhotra

I am thankful for many things every single day and I feel so much contentment. I feel blessed and lucky. I have more positive and constructive thoughts.

Fact: Thanking can heal your emotional wounds as well as illnesses/diseases!

"Of all the attitudes we can acquire, surely the attitude of gratitude is the most important, and by far the most life-changing." ~Zig Ziglar

When you look at the world, do you see much to be grateful for?

For every area of your life, how many things can you thank for?

Do you think once a year (thanksgiving day) is enough to thank for all that you have got?

Daily gratitude log

While you are working on your beliefs, thoughts, emotions and goals, it is also a good discipline to keep a blessings or gratitude journal. Get a little notebook and every night before going to sleep and first thing on waking in the morning, write down at least three things that you are grateful for or feel blessed to have in your life.

The more you can write down the better as this gets your thoughts focused on the good things you already have achieved. Doing it night and morning ensures that your mind is full of positive thoughts as you go to sleep and starts the day in a positive frame of mind.

Keep a gratitude journal. It is really good practice to recall the happy, joyful, funny or rewarding moments of your life often. Write them down and give thanks for them. Then if you are having a down day or you find another layer of the onion needs peeling, go back and read them.

Key no. 3 - **Contribution**

Do you contribute to the society? Do you give thanks for what you have and donate for/to the people in need?

I have been a volunteer for various charities and NPOs for the past few years. Whether its Polio immunization & AIDS awareness for the UNICEF or teaching life skills (mentioned in this book) to young orphans in India or the projects for the Red Cross, it has always been a nice experience and the main thing is that it *feels* nice!

When you donate to, or volunteer for a charity think about those disabled people, flood victims, earthquake survivors, education and food for deprived kids... people who would benefit from the money/material you gave or collected because the feelings/emotions you experience when you *contribute* are therapeutic. This experience also gives us a message that we are blessed and lucky and we are capable of making a difference hence a boost in our self-esteem.

> *"Service to others is the rent you pay for your room here on earth."*
> *~Muhammad Ali*

Do not contribute to show off or to satisfy your ego or to seek attention. It must come from your heart with pure joy and care. There are many ways you can contribute daily: put a smile on someone's face, lend a helping hand, make someone laugh, do little things which can keep this planet clean and safe... and these deeds don't cost a penny!

In today's life we experience more negative emotions than positive, how good would it feel to say 'I am able to help'? So, be kind and contribute. It's a win-win deal ☺

> *"Only those who have learned the power of sincere and selfless contribution experience life's deepest joy: true fulfilment."*
> *~Anthony Robbins*

"We all need to give back to society and people who do that should be acknowledged to keep them motivated." ~Katrina Kaif Turcotte
(Celebrated Actress, Philanthropist, Inspiring Role Model, Wax figure at Madame Tussauds London, Ambassador for UN's Global Goals Campaign)

Make a list of things you could do to contribute to the society, the planet and the people around you. Then set goals for it. Try to make it a part of your daily routine.

YOUR NOTES

A Very Important Message

If you don't answer the questions at the end of each chapter or don't create positive/healthy beliefs, you may never be able to live the life of your dreams!

I know of many readers who read this book and felt good or inspired but never did anything with what they learned!

Ask yourself: **What are my current beliefs/fears/habits costing me emotionally, physically and financially?**

What are the negative effects of my beliefs on my relationships, self-esteem and profession?

You will have to accept what is and then do something about it. No one will take action on your behalf!

Always keep in mind: **Past ≠ Future**

"In 20 years, you will be more disappointed by what you did not do than by what you did." ~Mark Twain

"Success seems to be connected with action. Successful people keep moving. They make mistakes, but they don't quit." ~Conrad Hilton

"You are free to choose, but you are not free from the consequences of your choice." ~Unknown

"I am not what happened to me. I am what I choose to become." ~Carl Jung

"Progress is impossible without change, and those who cannot change their minds cannot change anything." ~George Bernard Shaw

"Some people want it to happen, some wish it would happen, others make it happen." ~Michael Jordan

It's not about 'can' you, it's about 'will' you?

BONUS CHAPTERS

Ten Things the Most Successful, Happiest and Healthiest People Believe In and Do

Most of us are either unaware of these or not implementing them effectively.

Successful people from all walks of life have followed these principles to achieve what they wanted. Whether it's geniuses like Einstein or leaders like Gandhi, billionaires and entrepreneurs or Olympic gold medallists, Senior Managers of multi-nationals, hit singers, and Actors all of them have implemented these principles (many don't implement no.10 though!)

When I came across these facts I decided to consider, believe in and accept them because these have been, and still are, followed and implemented by the most successful, happy and healthy people. Initially it was hard for me to accept these and to delete my old beliefs but I did and my life changed, literally! (not overnight)

"When presented with a new idea, check your ego at the door and suspend your disbelief. Your ability to open your mind and consider new ideas without fear will propel you to the top faster than anything else."
~Bill Gove

1) They take responsibility for their lives

Rather than blaming everyone else for the problems in their lives the most successful people say 'I am responsible for my wealth, happiness and health'. They choose to construct their life and control their destiny. They accept themselves and their lives and take responsibility to make it better.

I had every reason to stay mediocre or average, to blame my circumstances, family, country and school but I realised that if I don't take responsibility for my life, accept myself and move forward then who else would! It dawned on me one day that I had to take massive action to make my life better because no one was coming to my rescue. Part of that massive action was my move to the UK.

How are you going to take responsibility for your life?

"In the long run, we shape our lives, and we shape ourselves. The process never ends until we die. And the choices we make are ultimately our own responsibility." ~Eleanor Roosevelt

"Success on any major scale requires you to accept responsibility. In the final analysis, the one quality that all successful people have is the ability to take responsibility." ~Michael Korda

"I am on a mission to live the best possible life. I am going to make the best of whatever situation I am in. I am still intact after all the tragedies and suffering I've been through. I've separated myself from the situation, learnt from it and moved forward." ~Hrithik Roshan
(Celebrated Actor, Ambassador for UNICEF's Global Education Campaign, Inspirational Youth Leader, Philanthropist, Wax figure at Madame Tussauds)

2) They develop empowering and successful beliefs

Successful people may not be more intelligent or talented than the rest but they believe they can be, do or have anything they want in life. They change attitudes and create habits which help them in making their lives better. They reprogram or recondition their mind for success in every area of their lives. They are not controlled by their fears. They challenge ideas and opinions, rather than just accept them as fact.

I had to get rid of my limiting beliefs and 'lack' programming before I started moving forward in life because they were big blocks which didn't let me see success or happiness. I had fear of failure and my self-confidence was very low. I didn't believe in my abilities. And all these negative beliefs made me stay poor, mediocre, unhappy and hate myself. But when I started to say and believe these three statements things my life started changing for good: 'I can', 'I deserve' and 'I am worthy'.

What happens in your life when you say 'I can', 'I deserve' and 'I am worthy'?

"Our beliefs about ourselves are the most telling factors in determining our level of success and happiness in life." ~Dr. Wayne Dyer

"The programming that you accept from others, and the conscious and unconscious directives, pictures, feelings and thoughts that you transmit to yourself, will find a place in your own internal control centre. Together, those thoughts and images will continue to create in advance or influence on the spot, every response, attitude and action that will be a part of you and your future." ~Dr. Shad Helmsletter

"If you believe you have the power to make your own luck, you will confidently engage in an action that will cause a positive change." ~Hrithik Roshan

3) They know thoughts become reality

They take responsibility of what they dwell on in their mind. They consciously choose to focus on successful, healthy and happy thoughts. They think big and believe in abundance not lack or scarcity. They are aware of the fact that what they repeat in their mind will become a belief. They keep track of their self-talk including the words they use.

I used to tell myself all kinds of negative things about myself. I used to stop myself from taking action by reminding myself of my failures in the past. I used lame words to describe myself, my abilities and my future. When I explored what I was repeating in my head I was shocked to discover I was reinforcing negative programming and was responsible for my unfulfilled life. I then created affirmations and vision boards to reprogram and focus my mind towards success.

What do you say to yourself? Do you like what you hear?

"They can… because they think they can." ~Virgil

"Men are not prisoners of fate, but only prisoners of their own minds."
~Franklin D. Roosevelt

"I have a very positive attitude in life. My insecurity and fears diminished as I worked on my mindset." ~Katrina Kaif Turcotte
(Celebrated Actress, Philanthropist, Inspiring Role Model, Wax figure at Madame Tussauds London, Ambassador for UN's Global Goals Campaign)

"If you want to test how powerful your mind is, simply start thinking positively and see the results for yourself." ~Maddy Malhotra

4) They understand the power of emotions

They know managing emotions is crucial for achieving success, happiness and wellness. Thoughts and beliefs trigger emotions so they make sure they have positive and fruitful thoughts as much as possible. They do things which make them happy, which make them laugh, make them feel healthy and which generate the feeling of love. They motivate themselves by emotions related to their dreams, desires and passion rather than by money and material possession.

Changing my beliefs raised my level of self-love. Feeling grateful gives me a sense of fulfilment. Meditation and relaxation gives me peace of mind and working for a purpose and mission gives me happiness. I spend few minutes every day watching or listening to something funny.

"The basic thing is that everyone wants happiness, no one wants suffering. And happiness mainly comes from our own attitude, rather than from external factors. If your own mental attitude is correct, even if you remain in a hostile atmosphere, you feel happy." ~Dalai Lama

5) They have a clear purpose/vision

They know what they want, why they want it and how to get it. They spend time on setting goals and creating action plans which will create the life of their dreams. They love what they do. They are bold and daring visionaries.

Somewhere within me I wasn't fulfilled. IT wasn't my passion, although it paid me well. But every morning I walked to work with emptiness in me and I just knew this isn't what I am supposed to do. By asking myself questions and by connecting with my inner-self I realised what my true passion was. I then started planning, dreaming and learning the skills required to fulfil and live my purpose.

Do you have a clear vision or purpose for your life? It doesn't need to be world-changing on a global scale – a vision of being the best parent you could be is world-changing enough.

"There is one quality one must possess to win, and that is definiteness of purpose, the knowledge of what one wants and a burning desire to possess it." ~Napoleon Hill

"I had big goals and I was very passionate, but I was not in a rush to grab anything to get there. I believed the right opportunities will unfold at the right time. It is a step by step journey. It is a process."
~Katrina Kaif Turcotte

6) They expect adversity and failure

They are driven to succeed, but unlike the majority they don't avoid mistakes, risks or failure. They don't seek security or comfort. They are criticised but are persistent. They choose discipline over pleasure.

Most people fool themselves by saying 'I work hard' or 'I am quite competent' or 'I am doing whatever I can' when in reality they aren't. The truth is that they have limiting beliefs about money and about what they can achieve or deserve. They want to live the 'rich' life but are unwilling to pay the price.

I was afraid of failure, of taking risk and wanted to have a better life whilst being comfortable. When I realised I was living in delusion I made up my mind to accept discomfort, to take calculated risks and to see the long term rewards. I had a choice to stay in India and live an average life or to migrate and have more freedom and growth opportunities. I had a choice to invest money in personal development or buying a house. I had a choice to keep working a high paying IT job or to work for my passion of helping others to make their life better. And for all these non-linear decisions of mine I was criticised and made fun of by my family, friends and colleagues!!

Warning! A lot of internet marketing, real estate and share trading trainers are selling people 'get rich quick with less effort' courses/products these days. Please be aware. Probably ask them how much time and energy did they spend to reach where they are ;-). The truth is that there is no 'quick' to getting rich!

"If you don't step out of your comfort zone and face your fears, the number of situations that make you uncomfortable will keep growing."
~Theo Pistorius

"To succeed in life one must have determination and must be prepared to suffer during the process. If one isn't prepared to suffer during adversities, I don't really see how he can be successful." ~Gary Player

"The more you practice overcoming your obstacles the more you will welcome them and be unafraid." ~Hrithik Roshan

7) They don't look for immediate rewards

This one goes hand in hand with no. 6 above. Unlike others they don't believe that compensation should instantly follow any effort. They know it can take years to manifest their ultimate vision, dream or goals. They focus on gratification which lasts rather than instant pleasure.

It took me almost two years to settle down in the UK. I could have started practicing life coaching, hypnotherapy or NLP soon after I completed the course but I first implemented it in my life so I could walk my talk. I could have taken a two-day course on public speaking and started my seminars but I opted for a year long course which is taught by the top 1% of speakers in the world. Believe it or not it can take the best professionals up to a year to prepare an hour long comedy show, speech or music performance!!

Can you delay the gratification of an instant success for a longer term more sustainable outcome?

"The key to everything is patience. You get the chicken by hatching the egg, not by smashing it." ~Arnold H. Glasgow

"Actually even at the beginning of my career, I never felt rejected. I was still working hard and believed in myself. I wasn't in a hurry and was picking and choosing projects carefully even then when I was just a newcomer. My attitude towards films hasn't changed even after these years." ~Katrina Kaif Turcotte

8) They have coaches and mentors. They are ever-ready learners.

They are committed to never ending personal and professional growth. They attend seminars and/or workshops and read books. They believe in working smarter not harder so they learn from the mentors or role-models that are the best in their fields which also helps them accelerate their performance. They have coaches for different areas of their lives. They invest time and money in getting better. For them failure is an opportunity to learn and grow.

I haven't stopped learning since I attended a personal development seminar a few years ago. I read books, I attend personal and professional development seminars often, I have three coaches for different areas of my life and I constantly apply this learning and suggest it to my clients.

Are you still green and growing, willing to learn?

"The most successful among us are not always the class valedictorians, but they are the best self-educated people on the planet." ~unknown

"I consider myself lucky to have worked with successful actors early on in my career because I got a chance to learn from them. You should not stop learning. I can't be the same person I was at 18, otherwise, I'd be stagnant. There is so much you can learn from the high achievers in any field."
~Katrina Kaif Turcotte

9) They take care of their physical fitness, nutrition and relaxation

They understand physical activity is a must and it has numerous benefits both emotionally, mentally and physically. They consciously choose what they eat, when they eat and how much they eat. They make time to relax their body and mind because they know we aren't robots.

"Honor the physical temple that houses you by eating healthfully, exercising, listening to your body's needs, and treating it with dignity and love." ~Dr. Wayne Dyer

I had no clue about nutrition and was very lazy until a few years ago. I used to spend a lot of my time watching TV and chatting on the phone. I was surprised to see the effects of regular exercise on my mind and body. My immune system is far better since I started taking care of my diet.

Do you take care of your body – or expect it to take care of you?

"Exercise is king, nutrition is queen, but together you have the entire kingdom!" ~Jack Lalanne

"To me fitness is very important and the primary factor is that I feel better. Like a lot of us, I was really lazy and used to find excuses for not going to the gym. It's not only about the way you look and aesthetics; it's about the way you feel. When you are fit you feel healthy, you look better and you function better." ~Katrina Kaif Turcotte
(Celebrated Actress, Listed 4 times in FHM 100 Sexiest Women in the World)

10) They forgive and are grateful

They know a lack of forgiveness can block dreams and goals from manifesting in every area of life.

"We achieve inner health only through forgiveness - the forgiveness not only of others but also of ourselves" ~Joshua Liebman

They are grateful for what they have. This not only gives them a sense of fulfilment it also increases their self-esteem and confidence. A biological benefit of this is that the brain releases useful chemicals during this process of expressing gratitude.

Until I went through the process of forgiving others and myself I was sabotaging my peace of mind, happiness and success. I was full of blames, complains, resentment and lack. Being grateful for what I already have and what I achieve in my day-to-day life gives me inner joy.

Are you grateful for everything you have, everything you have achieved and everything that is yet to come?

"It is necessary to cultivate the habit of being grateful for every good thing that comes to you, and to give thanks continuously." ~Wallace Wattles

"I believe that if you reject and don't respect what you have now, that's ingratitude. I am grateful for everything I have today."
~Katrina Kaif Turcotte

YOUR NOTES

Effective Parenting

Most parents aren't aware of how life works and unconsciously program their kids to be average/failures

YES, you read it right. No matter what country it is, most of the parents don't know how the mind works and the fact that they program their kid's mind every single day. As I have mentioned in the previous chapters that it's the programming in the first few years of our lives which decides how much successful and happy we will be (the next chapter will detail the role of teachers/school in programming the mind of the students)

We are programmed to believe that parents are right, teachers are right, religious leaders are right and in some cases the celebrities are right… that's NOT true! They may be our well wishers BUT most of them are NOT aware of how life works and how to make life successful and happy because they were never taught/told and they never tried to learn…

The fact is that more than 90% of the people in the world have emotional issues or have a low self-esteem or are middle-class or poor. WHY? They never learn the principles of Success and Happiness!!

Every major religion has documented this fact that parenting and schooling should be done very carefully. Science has also proven this in the past few decades. From the time we are in the womb we are programmed by our parent(s) or guardians. Not just that, a child could be prone to many diseases if the parents experience negative emotions regularly while s/he is in the womb!

> *"Beyond any doubt, parents have overwhelming influence on the mental and physical attributes of the children they raise." ~Dr. Thomas Verny*

Parenting must be done consciously because the child listens to everything the parents say and even before understanding the language the child observes everything happening around and stores it in her/his mind. As a result her/his parents' beliefs and behaviour become their own.

You will be surprised to know that just one scolding or punishment or blame done with high emotional intensity can wound a child's self-esteem forever!! That child may always think of her/himself as unworthy or inferior or undeserving!

"No child ever became 'good' by being told that she or he was bad or by beating her/him." ~Maddy Malhotra

A lot of parents think that just providing food, shelter and good education to their child is enough and their duty ends there. It is NOT true. We are emotional creatures. We need constant praise, we need someone to believe in us, we need someone to support us no matter what, we need lots of love. But these days parents rarely give unconditional love and praise. A child has to perform in order to get love. In some countries a child has to make parents happy by achieving good scores and medals to get their parent's attention/praise. Would you call this a happy family or a give and take relationship?

"Those children who are beaten will in turn give beatings, those who are intimidated will be intimidating, those who are humiliated will impose humiliation, and those whose souls are murdered will murder."
~Alice Miller

It is possible to reprogram the genes if the parents are conscious while bringing up a child. Effective parenting can make a child's life successful and happy.

Right or wrong, to do or not to do, love something or hate it, which religion and traditions must be followed and which shouldn't be... where did you learn/adopt all this from? Did you analyse and decide yourself? In most cases NO you didn't. You were programmed to judge/filter things and people by your parents and other authority figures.

"Freedom is not worth having if it does not include the freedom to make mistakes." ~Mahatma Gandhi

Parents (and couples planning to produce a baby) must invest time in reading personal development and parenting books and in attending workshops/seminars. Parents can make sure that their child's school's curriculum includes mindset/psychology related material and creativity enhancement activities in the curriculum.

Think how would it feel if you were praised and told that you can achieve big things, you can opt for the career that your heart desires, you future will be full of happiness, peace and love? Think how would the world be if parents take the responsibility of their child's programming? Think how much happier, wealthier and healthier the next generations will be...

Fact: Your low self-esteem and emotional states affect your kids and their perceptions. Your negative energy poisons the overall happiness of the family.

*if you want to explore how you can implement this for your kids to live a happy and successful life then email me: parenting@coachmaddy.com

Are you living your life or what your parents wanted you to become?

The fears, the beliefs, the doubts you have in your mind about your success are real or defined by your parents?

(if you have a child) Are you a responsible/conscious parent?

(if you are planning to have a child) Are you ready to learn and implement the facts of life before programming a little innocent being?

Do We Need Only Professional Education?

Most schools and teachers don't prepare us to create a happy life.

Most teachers today are just masters of theoretical subjects and not real Gurus who show the path of success/happiness/love/peace to their students because schools these days prepare us for professional competency NOT life skills. However, it's not their fault because they weren't taught anything else except technical theory.

Today's school life is full of competition, comparison, scolding, becoming perfect and at many schools beating is still thought to be a tool for betterment without thinking about the negative affect on students' self-worth, confidence, self-image and generating negative emotions like hatred, anger, jealousy, anxiety and depression within them!!

"An educational system isn't worth a great deal if it teaches young people how to make a living but doesn't teach them how to make a life."
~Unknown

"To many children, school represents a "second chance" -an opportunity to acquire a better sense of self and a better vision of life than was offered in their home. A teacher who projects confidence in a child's competence and goodness can be a powerful antidote to a family in which such confidence is lacking and in which perhaps the opposite perspective is conveyed. A teacher who treats boys and girls with respect can provide enlightenment for a child struggling to understand human relationships who comes from a home where such respect is nonexistent. A teacher who refuses to accept a child's negative self-concept and relentlessly holds to a better view of the child's potential has the power-sometimes-to save a life."
~Dr. Nathaniel Branden

If teachers are limited thinkers, if teachers don't know how the mind works, if teachers believe that the students who score good marks are the ones who will be successful and happy then what would the students be programmed for? What will happen to the confidence of the average performers? What will happen to the self-esteem of the students who fail exams? Teachers, like parents, must be very careful about what they say to their students in regards to their performance and while judging/predicting their future.

"The only person who is educated is the one who has learned how to learn and change." ~Carl Rogers

When we know that every minute of our lives are affected by our Thoughts, Emotions, Beliefs then why isn't the psychology of success and happiness a part of our secondary school, college and university curriculum? Why is our primary education focused only on professional and social success?

Are the curriculum designers successful and happy leaders/visionaries or just degree holders?

Is the education system moving pupils away from happiness? Children are being programmed for competition from an early age. They are completely poisoned when they graduate and leave university. They learn that life is the survival of the fittest instead of celebration. Rather than teaching cooperation, schools teach to compete and be at the top. There is very little or no training for love, bliss and creativity. In fact, there is no guarantee of bliss/joy, even when someone is a top performer. Students turn into professionals and go through a lot of misery to reach that place. Anxiety and stress become part of their lifestyle because they don't know any other way. Schools must help the students to use the right brain, develop creativity and teach them to pursue what their hearts desire.

Is it more important for us to know who created which mathematical theorem OR is it more important to learn how to add wealth, happiness and love and how to subtract negative emotions?

Is it more important for us to know the science of planets and sea life OR is it more important to learn the science of generating wealth, happiness and love?

Is it more important for us to know who did what 200 years ago OR is it more important to learn how to be rich, happy and healthy in the next 20 years?

"We want that education by which character is formed, strength of mind is increased, the intellect is expanded, and by which one can stand on one's own feet." ~Swami Vivekananda

A lot of high achievers either weren't good at academics or don't have degrees but they are ever-ready learners. They learned the principles of success, took control of their beliefs, followed their passion and made it to the top.

"In education we tend to turn out conformists, stereotypes, individuals whose education is 'completed,' rather than freely creative and original thinkers." ~Carl Rogers

At universities (and teaching hospitals), millions are being spent on research for curing illnesses but nothing is spent to educate people about the power of mind and how our negative emotions create illnesses! Which means very less or nothing is being done to deal with the root cause while we are busy dealing with the effects…!

"In medical school, we have a hundred classes that teach us how to fight off death and not one lesson in how to go on living." ~Dr. Meredith Grey

*If you or your school is interested in implementing the above then email me: teaching@coachmaddy.com

Am I a role model for my students or just a theory teacher?

Am I a leader or an authoritarian?

Do I praise and see good in every student or just the high scorers?

Do I support/help my students to raise their self-esteem?

Ancient Wisdom for Success and Happiness

What do the religions say about the power of mind

Every major religion whether it's Christianity, Buddhism, Hinduism, or Islam has mentioned the power of mind for various things such as:

✓ Our Thoughts/Intentions become reality
✓ Positive emotions such as Happiness, Peace and Love come from within and can be experienced at will
✓ Negative emotions are our choice and can create physical illnesses and problems in multiple areas of life

Socrates, Lao Tzu, Yogananda, Gandhi, Einstein or Mother Teresa… in the past few centuries the great leaders, enlightened saints/gurus, and philosophers believed and implemented this.

Few examples with my interpretations:

"As a man thinketh in his heart so is he"
Meaning: we become what we think about
(Proverbs 23:7 – Holy Bible)

"And all things, whatsoever ye shall ask in prayer, <u>believing</u>, ye shall receive."
(Matthew 21:22 – Holy Bible, 2000+ years ago)

"We are what we think. All that we are arises with our thoughts. With our thoughts we make our world."
(Buddha, 3000+ years ago)

"Amal ka daromadar niyaton per hai"
Meaning: Your intentions lead to actions (and results)
(Al-amara, Muslim sharif, 1400+ years ago)

"Jaisa socho gay waisay bana diye jao gay"
Meaning: You will be made whatever you think
(Hadith, Sahih Bukhari)

"Bandhur atmatmanas tasya yenatmaivatmana jitah, anatmanas tu satrutve vartetatmaiva satruvat"
Meaning: for him who has conquered the mind, the mind is the best of friends; but for one who has failed to do so, his mind will be the greatest enemy!
(Bhagvad Geeta 6.6 - Hinduism, 3500+ years ago)

Today's philosophers call it the Law of Attraction or the Law of Cause & Effect (karma)

God never said that you will live an average life or an unfulfilled life. You and the people who programmed your mind 'assumed' your worth, ability and deserving-ness. You have the same brains and ability like the most successful ones have. Only the circumstances are different and I can assure you that your circumstances are not the worst.

God is full of love, joy and peace. Every religion has said that God is within us or we are a part of God so why do we think small? Why do we have limiting beliefs about our success? Why do we not love ourselves? Why do we have fears? Why don't we trust our intuition? Isn't thinking negative/small a sin then?

Every major religion also documents the fact that we ourselves have to take action to achieve whatever we desire. So why leave it on luck when your thoughts, faith and actions create your destiny?

"The religious books mentioned about the 'power of mind' thousands of years ago, so why do you have to wait until the science proves it in the 21st century? Let others wait to realise/prove the facts, not you."
~Maddy Malhotra

Another thing which surprises me is that most of the religious people don't read and understand their religious documents properly/fully and rarely follow the core messages. They just follow the rules which they have learned from their elders and religious leaders. These rules usually are 'physical' practices rather than true faith/connection i.e. the non-tangible part of the religion which is the most important part. And without implementing the 'mental/emotional' practices they complain that God/Almighty doesn't answer their prayers... awkward isn't it?

Explore Yourself (if you are religious)

Ask yourself:

Do I follow the rules which were created to make life happier, peaceful, love-full and meaningful or am I stuck in implementing the rules by which others judge me?

Have I ever tried to find out why those rules were made/given by God or do I just follow them because I was programmed to follow? (although to understand any religion completely, you will have to understand the concepts including: parapsychology, life after death, roles of good and bad supernatural beings on earth, your energy body, intuition, laws of the universe, difference between the universal super power and the avatars of God / son of God)

Congratulations!

You have now taken those first great steps towards living the life you dream of and deserve. Your good wolf's belly will be growing in contentment for finally you are feeding it with positive beliefs, empowering self-talk and joyous emotions.

When you need help to take the next steps to happiness, fulfillment, joy, wealth and wellness, then contact me and I will be your guide. Whether you would like me to work with you as your personal coach or you would prefer my home study guide (or both!), I will be very happy to help you on your journey.

I wish you a Wealthier, Happier, Love-filled, Healthier and Peaceful life!

Maddy

Maddy Malhotra ☺

www.CoachMaddy.com

IT'S MY CHOICE *by Maddy Malhotra*

I get a gift every morning, the gift of a new day,

It's up to me whether I make it bright, joyful or grey.

I can choose to be Happy, Successful and Content,

Or dishonour it with worry, anger or resent.

The next steps with Maddy

Home Study Course *(based on this book)*

Would you like to feel better about yourself than ever before? Would you like to see yourself producing better results? Would you like to feel more fulfilled in your work, your relationships and your life?

My home study course has helped many people around the world to achieve one or more results listed below. It will help you work on your beliefs, emotions, thoughts and self-talk, and help you achieve every goal you set yourself *without fail*.

The home study course can help you get rid of:
- ✖ Limiting/negative beliefs
- ✖ Fear of failure
- ✖ Low self-esteem
- ✖ Lack of self-confidence
- ✖ A feeling of not being good enough
- ✖ Negative self image
- ✖ Feeling 'unlucky'
- ✖ Procrastination
- ✖ Lack of fulfilment and peace of mind
- ✖ Negative attitude
- ✖ Unwanted/unhealthy habits

You will learn in detail:
- ➢ How to change your limiting beliefs
- ➢ How to create new empowering beliefs and techniques to really embed and support them
- ➢ How to change and manage your emotions
- ➢ How to change your self-talk and daily thoughts to support your new beliefs
- ➢ How to set goals in such a way that you can't fail to achieve them

The home study course will help you understand WHY you have problems or barriers in any given area of life and provide you with PROVEN tools and techniques to help you get rid of problems and make your life better. The course provides both the theory behind all these techniques and why they work, and exercises for you to put these techniques into practise for yourself, bullet-proofing your self-belief.

On completing the home study course you will have rock solid self belief so that <u>you can</u>

✓ Achieve any goal you set (e.g. for increasing your income, achieving your ideal body shape, building high self esteem, happier relationships or anything else)
✓ Feel confident about yourself
✓ Unleash your true potential and achieve peak performance
✓ Make better decisions for yourself
✓ Feel good about yourself and your achievements
✓ Focus on the positive things in your life and manifest more of them
✓ Be more of the person you want to be
✓ Take control of your emotional reactions

Get yours now!!!

To get started on **<u>creating a successful and happy life</u>** with the home study course go to www.CoachMaddy.com or email homestudy@coachmaddy.com to receive a **$20** discount voucher!

One to One Coaching

If you are committed to make your life better then I will help you to change your limiting beliefs, thoughts and self talk, support you to set goals and hold you accountable whilst fully believing in you, so <u>you can</u>

- ✓ **Progress** in your **career** or business

- ✓ **Gain confidence** and improve your **self-image**/esteem

- ✓ **Feel good** by achieving your **ideal body shape**

- ✓ Have **fulfilling relationships** and have **more time** for your family and yourself

- ✓ **Achieve** your **goals** and follow through your intentions

- ✓ **Increase** your **income** to **enjoy** the luxuries you wish

- ✓ Have a **positive attitude**. Make better decisions.

- ✓ Achieve **peak performance**

- ✓ Be a **good parent** (ensure your child's happy and successful life)

- ✓ **Be in control** of your reactions

- ✓ Experience more **happiness, peace** and **fulfillment**

When you are ready to develop your own bullet-proof self beliefs, then email me with some details of what you would like to achieve: success@coachmaddy.com or read more details about my coaching services on: www.CoachMaddy.com

YOU CHOOSE *by Maddy Malhotra*

Birth wasn't your choice,

And neither shall death be.

But the way you live your life

Is your choice, buddy.

Join Maddy

For inspirational quotes, media interviews, personal development articles and videos, book updates and discussions: <u>read and subscribe</u>:

BLOG   www.CoachMaddy.com

f   /maddymfanpage

/coachmaddym

/coachmaddy

g   www.Goodreads.com
(more than 100 quotes by Maddy)

Media Personnel

For interviews, articles and releases
email: media@coachmaddy.com
You may visit my website for more details www.CoachMaddy.com

Bloggers / Book Reviewers

For book reviews, free copies of the book and interviewing me
email: blogs@coachmaddy.com

Charity / NPO

We always donate a part of our earnings. For <u>fundraising</u> through book sales, our workshops or other ways please email:
charity@coachmaddy.com

Suggested Reading

Once you understand the concepts and principles listed in this book you may want to know more about life.

'My heart says..', 'my gut feeling..', 'inner-guidance' are some of the words we use for intuition. Whether it's Steve Jobs or Gandhi, Albert Einstein or Mother Teresa, myself or any other bestselling author, best painters or movie makers... they all value(d) and act(ed) upon the messages they get/got via their intuition.

A good book for understanding the facts like:

- ✓ Intuition
- ✓ Laws of the Universe
- ✓ Energy / Vibration / Frequency
- ✓ Relationships at soul level

"Your Life: A Practical Guide to Happiness, Peace and Fulfilment" by Hina Hashmi (Clinical Psychologist and Empowerment Coach)

YOUR NOTES

YOUR NOTES

CPSIA information can be obtained
at www.ICGtesting.com
Printed in the USA
LVHW040750140819
627605LV00005B/154